THE BUILDING BLOCKS OF BELONGING

5 STEPS TO CREATING A MORE DIVERSE, EQUITABLE, AND INCLUSIVE CULTURE

ANDREW ADENIYI
CEO & FOUNDER OF AAA SOLUTIONS

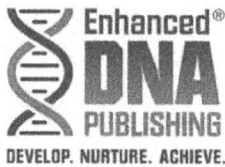

Enhanced®
DNA
PUBLISHING
DEVELOP. NURTURE. ACHIEVE.

DenolaBurton@EnhancedDNA1.com
www.EnhancedDNAPublishing.com
317-250-5611

The Building Blocks of Belonging

5 Steps to Creating a Diverse, Equitable, and Inclusive
Culture

ISBN: 979-8-9889738-7-4

Library of Congress: 2024901361

INTRODUCTION

9 minutes and 29 seconds...the length of time former Minneapolis Police Officer, Derek Chauvin, held his knee to the neck of George Floyd on May 25, 2020. This senseless act of murder, not only led to Chauvin going to prison, it sparked a worldwide social justice movement unlike anything ever seen before. Millions took to the streets to march and protest police brutality and other systemic injustices crippling America.

The impact of Floyd's death sent shockwaves throughout companies and organizations as well. CEOs and senior leaders scrambled to send a message to their teams and stakeholders. Suddenly, every leader's #1 priority became the safety and well-being of their teams, with special consideration on Black, Indigenous, and Persons of Color (BIPOC) team members.

I was personally, deeply impacted by this event. Although countless minorities have been unnecessarily killed by police officers, none brought me to tears like the murder of George Floyd. I was broken by learning that it started with an alleged counterfeit bill being used at a nearby small business, the nonchalant demeanor Chauvin displayed as Floyd yelled for his deceased mother, and the nine minutes and twenty-nine damn seconds that a knee was on the neck of an unarmed black man! Chauvin would not move his knee until forced to by paramedics.

That series of events, coupled with the fact I could watch the entire thing on video, made me cry like I hadn't in years. In the past, I would feel numb when something like this happened. With this situation, I felt violated, disrespected, infuriated, and powerless. This book is the product of those tears. The culmination of me realizing that my purpose and my passion is to inspire others specifically through the lens of diversity, equity, and inclusion as well as workplace culture.

My hope is that this book will empower leaders, HR professionals, and entrepreneurs to create environments that are diverse, equitable, and inclusive. This book is for leaders who want their team members to feel engaged and have a sense of belonging in their place of work. If you fit any of the descriptions above, this book is for you.

Regardless of whether your organization does not currently have an effective DEI strategy or possess the knowledge, tools, and resources to take your DEI strategy to the next level, this book provides the building blocks necessary to elevate your organizational culture from awareness to accountability.

After hours of focused and intentional research, interviews, and practical application, I have created a DEI model that small to medium sized business leaders can implement starting today. The model is what I refer to as the "Building Blocks of Belonging". I validated this concept by first asking the question: what is the result of an effective DEI strategy? My answer? An engaged workforce where diversity of thought is encouraged, psychological safety is prioritized, and a culture of belonging is fostered.

Before I give you the overview of the building blocks, let me share why I believe I am credible to deliver this message.

1. As a 6'1, 215-pound, first-generation Nigerian American who has studied at predominantly white institutions (PWI) while a member of a historically black fraternity also known as the oldest and coldest to ever do it, (Alpha Phi Alpha, Fraternity, Inc.), I live DEI daily.
2. Working in retail management for almost a dozen years, I have crossed paths with a diverse group of leaders, teams, and people.
3. As a consultant, leadership junkie, speaker, and published author, I have the education, experience, and passion to "be at

the podium". I feel uniquely equipped to add value to others through the lens of workplace culture and DEI. This is the moment where I park at the intersection of my passion and expertise in order to solve a problem in the marketplace. There is power in walking in your purpose. This book is me picking up the mic.

The 5 building blocks start with *Cultivating Culture* which is all about prioritizing your organization's purpose and defining key terms around DEI. Part 2 tackles *Emotional Intelligence (EQ)* and *Psychological Safety* which covers self-awareness, empathy, and vulnerability in the workplace. Part 3 aims at answering the question, what are *Biases and Micro-aggressions* and how can we disrupt those biases towards various underrepresented groups? Part 4 covers *Conflict Resolution* and how to have a courageous conversation. Lastly, Part 5 will help you ensure consistent equity in the workplace through *Activating Allyship* and holding yourself and others accountable in fostering a sense of belonging for ALL.

Each chapter will include quotes, stories, research, and practical application. If you are still wondering why implementing or improving your DEI strategy is so important, look at these statistics...

Recruiting, retaining, and advancing diverse top talent is critical to remaining competitive. According to Deloitte, companies with inclusive cultures have:

- 22 percent lower turnover rates
- 22 percent greater productivity
- 27 percent higher profitability
- 39 percent higher customer satisfaction

I trust you will read, reflect, implement, and share.

Enjoy,

Andrew Adeniyi

Andrew Adeniyi

TABLE OF CONTENTS

THE BUILDING BLOCKS OF BELONGING

5 STEPS TO CREATING A DIVERSE, EQUITABLE, AND INCLUSIVE CULTURE

BY ANDREW ADENIYI

ACTIVATING ALLYSHIP

RESOLVING CONFLICT

DISRUPTING BIAS & MICRO-AGGRESSIONS

DEVELOPING EMOTIONAL INTELLIGENCE & PSYCHOLOGICAL SAFETY

CULTIVATING CULTURE & PRIORITIZING PURPOSE

CHAPTER 1: CULTIVATING CULTURE: PRIORITIZING PURPOSE

The first building block is about prioritizing purpose and answering the question "why?". During this phase, I will walk you through how to create and leverage a compelling vision statement, mission statement, and set of core values from which a DEI purpose will be born. Key terms around DEI are defined during this phase and the value proposition for DEI in the workplace is explored.

Amplifying Purpose

"Values matter most in times of crisis." I first heard this quote from former Starbucks CEO, Kevin Johnson. I was working for Starbucks at the time and found the quote pertinent as the company, and the world, were in crisis.

The abrupt and violent emergence of Covid-19 in March of 2020 turned the world upside down and brought a level of disruption and fear not seen in decades. Decisions on closing or opening stores to prioritize the health and safety of customers and partners (employees) weighed heavily on the leaders of the organization.

However, just as Kevin stated, times of crisis are ideal moments to lean heavily on your organizational purpose (i.e., mission statement, vision, core values). When it was time for Starbucks to decide how to navigate this crisis, they used their mission and values as guiding principles. Their mission of inspiring and nurturing the human spirit became the compass that guided the organization forward amid darkness and ambiguity.

Starbucks responded by committing to cultivating a culture of belonging. Here are some examples of ways they prioritized their purpose:

- Paid partners, even if they did not feel safe to go into work
- Provided free mental health support for all partners through a provider called Lyra
- Continued to pay bonuses despite business challenges
- Over communicated with the team through email, internal channels, and video calls
- Solicited feedback from partners within the company regularly and took action around the feedback collected

These actions amplified their mission of inspiring and nurturing the human spirit. In my book, *The Circle of Leadership*, I outline some examples of how powerful cultivating culture can be. Specifically, when we break down culture and purpose, it comes down to clarifying your vision. What is your 10-year goal? What does success look like down the road if you exceed your wildest imagination for your goals? These are questions that start pointing you in the direction of your vision.

Mission refers to what you do, how you do it, and why you do it. For example, the mission of my organization is to help leaders create more engaged, diverse, equitable, and inclusive cultures. By focusing on this mission daily, we will move closer to our goal (the vision) for my firm, which is to become the largest black-owned DEI consulting firm in the Midwest by 2030. The "why" behind this statement is to leverage our size to begin improving workplaces across the world. The clarity of this vision and mission helps us make decisions.

Preserve the Core, Stimulate Progress

The last piece of organizational purpose is core values. At AAA Solutions, our values are simplicity, autonomy, and growth. These guiding principles influence hiring, incentivizing, and firing team members. Values provide a universal lens for an organization to view its work. For example, at AAA Solutions, when we are faced with a complex issue, we look for ways to simplify our problem. The value of simplicity invites us always to seek ways to make things easier.

When interviewing, asking questions about how candidates have approached simplifying things in the past helps us infuse our values into our business. During performance reviews, you reinforce the importance of your core values by asking for examples of processes or systems that a team member has made more efficient. Terminating team members who consistently do not align with the organization's core values is also important. Employees need to know that alignment with core values is an integral part of being a part of the team.

When it comes to organizational culture, there are three main ways to categorize environments: Task vs. Purpose-Driven, Collaborative vs. Competitive, and Status Quo vs. Innovate. Let's break down each section:

1. **Task vs. Purpose-Driven:** Task-driven environments are very checklist-heavy, compliance-oriented, and top-down leadership centric. Purpose-driven environments are where team members are inspired by a common mission, vision, and values.
2. **Competitive vs. Collaborative:** Competitive environments are highly independent, whereas collaborative environments are highly integrated team efforts.
3. **Status Quo vs. Innovate**: Status quo environments live by the motto, "If it ain't broke, don't fix it." These environments are highly predictable and stable. On the other hand, innovative environments are highly flexible and encourage failing fast. Innovative cultures understand the importance of quickly adapting to change.

In the article, "Note on Organizational Culture", by the Stanford

Graduate School of Business, describes the relationship between strong cultures and performance. The article highlights the significant amount of empirical research "that suggests that organizational cultures play a crucial role in shaping the capabilities of organizations and guiding the behavior of individuals within organizations."

The article concluded that strong corporate cultures, where "basic assumptions of the culture are widely shared and deeply held by members of the organization", lead to higher performance and more consistency. Strong performance coupled with less volatility helps these firms sustain a competitive advantage in the marketplace.

Below are the three reasons why strong-culture firms out-perform weak-culture firms:

1. **Social Control:** When firms implement strong cultures, the norms of the culture help positively influence behavior. In fact, research shows that in companies with a strong culture, "corrective" actions are more likely to come from other employees, regardless of their place in the formal hierarchy. Therefore, informal social control is likely cheaper and more effective than formal control structures."

2. **Decision-Making:** In a body of work titled "Corporate Culture and Economic Theory," author David M. Kreps, shared that "goal alignment also facilitates coordination, as there is less room for debate between different parties about the firm's best interests." When firms have strong corporate cultures in place, there tends to be better clarity around goals and decision-making. These characteristics are especially helpful when ambiguity is present in the workplace because efficiency is still captured by employees being able to make sound decisions in the face of uncertainty.

3. **Employee Engagement:** Firms with strong cultures tend to have actively engaged and motivated employees. This sense of motivation and direction inspires employees, which creates a

better atmosphere for accomplishing goals. In an article titled "Corporations, Culture and Commitment: Motivation and Social Control in Organizations," author Charles A. O'Reilly stated, "Strong cultures can enhance employee motivation and performance due to the perception that behavior is more freely chosen." The autonomy that often comes with strong corporate cultures allows for higher levels of engagement.

Why DEI?

Diversity, equity, and inclusion (DEI) is a subset of workplace culture. So, before you dive into DEI, you must understand the larger umbrella that DEI falls under. Power is unlocked when a group of people prioritize purpose and cultivate culture. This is why understanding the value of a healthy workplace culture is vital.

One of the first questions I ask CEOs and executive leaders when they express interest in my firm's DEI consulting and training services is, "Why do you want to prioritize DEI?" This is an important question and one that we all must take time to answer. Victor Frankl, a Holocaust survivor, once said that "when you know your why, you can endure almost any how". That is how powerful a why can be. It provides direction and determination in the face of everything that follows.

Let's examine the following scenario as an example. If a workplace that embraces diversity of thought and fosters a sense of belonging results in a diverse, equitable, and inclusive culture, the question then becomes, "Why does diversity, equity and inclusion matter to you as a leader?" Let's say one of your personal core values is innovation. When you feel a sense of belonging at work, it is likely that you will be more engaged and, therefore, relatively productive. A few key ingredients to experiencing a sense of belonging is trust and safety. When you believe that an environment is safe, it enables you to have a sense of trust which is foundational for innovating.

Navigating Burnout

Cultivating a culture where purpose is prioritized helps mitigate burnout. According to "Managing Burnout: 3 Ways to Support Employee Wellbeing", an article by Culture Amp, burnout is "a syndrome conceptualized as resulting from chronic workplace stress that has not been successfully managed." Burnout is associated with energy depletion, disconnection from work, and lower performance, which ultimately impacts employee engagement and retention.

According to Culture Amp, they compared employee survey responses to the statement "I rarely feel overstressed by my work" with their engagement data. Dr. Roza Jankovic, Senior People Scientist at Culture Amp, said, "If they're responding favorably that they don't have stress, they're 89.5% engaged. For those who strongly disagree – those who are feeling overly stressed – they're only 39.7% engaged. So, you can start to see that burnout does impact employee engagement."

With burnout being a cancer to workplaces, leaders must be intentional with managing burnout to maximize their team's performance. A few keys for leaders looking to reduce burnout are:

- Create a culture of giving and receiving feedback. When people at work feel safe to provide feedback, they most likely feel respected and valued at work, which will help them navigate burnout more effectively. When there is a culture in the organization of soliciting feedback and acting once feedback is received, the level of trust in the organization is higher than in companies that do not have that culture.

- Improve the emotional intelligence of all people leaders in the organization. Emotional intelligence is all about understanding and managing your emotions as well as the emotions of others. To mitigate burnout, you must be able to recognize the signs of burnout so you can address it in a timely fashion. Empathy is the most critical component of emotional intelligence as it pertains specifically to one's ability to put themselves in another person's shoes. Leaders must be intentional with growing their ability to demonstrate empathy at work.

Remote & Hybrid Culture

Remote and hybrid cultures present unique challenges for leaders looking to cultivate culture and prioritize purpose. There is nothing like meeting face-to-face and being able to observe body language in a more intimate way. However, there are ways to create and elevate workplace culture even when the entire team is not in the same room.

According to an article by Harvard Business Review, a few things leaders can do to foster a healthy workplace culture are:

- Focus on clear and consistent communication.
- Leverage symbols, artifacts, and organization-wide rituals
- Equip the team with resources and tools needed to thrive in a hybrid and/or remote environment.

I once heard that before someone can understand what you say to them, you must tell them what you are going to say, say what you have to say, and then tell them what you just told them. The takeaway from this mindset is that we must over-communicate to people before the message really sinks in.

This strategy is also important for cultivating culture, especially in a remote/hybrid environment. When all parties are not simultaneously present in the same physical space, ensuring equal access to key information is important so that some do not feel disconnected and neglected. Sustained feelings of being excluded are the exact opposite of the work we are trying to accomplish when it comes to DEI.

Intentionality in the areas of symbols, artifacts, and organization-wide rituals allows collaboration to thrive. These re-occurring cultural components influence behavior and align a team around the company's overall direction. Increasing employee morale and ownership is another expected outcome of doing this well.

Lastly, people leave jobs for better opportunities to grow. Therefore, it is paramount that leaders understand the wants and needs of their team so they can meet or exceed those needs. This level of intentionality allows you to examine what tools, resources, and training the team needs to perform to the best of their ability. A question to ask your team is "How can we foster interaction, better conversations, and effective collaboration between departments in a hybrid work environment?" The answer to that question will help you head in the right direction.

Managing Change

As you self-reflect, evaluate your <u>learning agility</u> and ability to manage change. According to The Center for Creative Leadership, "Tips for Improving Your Learning Agility", learning agility is about "learning from experience and applying it in new ways, adapting to new circumstances and opportunities." These concepts play a big role in the stress and/or success you experience while managing a remote/hybrid workforce.

THE EQUATION FOR CHANGE

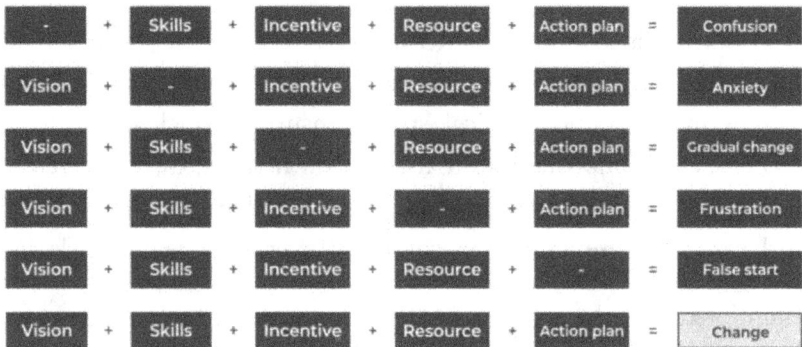

—	+ Skills	+ Incentive	+ Resource	+ Action plan	=	Confusion
Vision	+ —	+ Incentive	+ Resource	+ Action plan	=	Anxiety
Vision	+ Skills	+ —	+ Resource	+ Action plan	=	Gradual change
Vision	+ Skills	+ Incentive	+ —	+ Action plan	=	Frustration
Vision	+ Skills	+ Incentive	+ Resource	+ —	=	False start
Vision	+ Skills	+ Incentive	+ Resource	+ Action plan	=	Change

modified, originally from Beckhard-Harris "Dissatisfaction" model

To successfully manage change, you must start with understanding the why behind the change. The change equation breaks down all the components needed to adapt to change which includes:

- Vision (Why the change matters and why now)
- Skills (Confidence in the ability to adapt to change)
- Incentive (Motivation for adhering to the change)
- Resource (Tools needed to effectively manage change)
- Action Plan (Roadmap for achieving the desired result)

As the change equation shows, failure to not adopt any one of these components can lead to confusion, anxiety, gradual change, frustration, and/or a false start with your change initiative. By asking yourself what is important to you and intentionally connecting the dots between your personal purpose and the purpose of DEI at work, you will likely find the alignment needed to commit to DEI.

The business case for diversity in the workplace is clear. For example, "The Other Diversity Dividend," an article from HBR, highlights how, in the venture capital industry, "diversity significantly improves financial performance on measures such as profitable investments at the individual portfolio-company level and overall fund returns." However, to truly commit to DEI work, the reasoning must be on an individual level and be deeper than business.

Although it is a human tendency to associate with people like us, diversity brings together our uniqueness to create something much more dynamic than what we could achieve alone. The lived experiences, diversity of perspectives, and collaboration and innovation that can stem from DEI must all be top of mind before we dive into the remaining portions of the Building Blocks of Belonging.

Here are 3 things to do as you reflect on the content of this chapter:

1. Identify your top 3-5 core values. Review why you selected those core values and what they each mean to you.

2. Determine how DEI aligns with at least one of your core values. Be sure to truly believe in the intersection of your values and what DEI can provide in a workplace.

3. Create at least one Smart, Measurable, Attainable, Relative, Time-sensitive (SMART) goal for yourself centered around taking tangible action to foster a better sense of belonging at work.

In summary, you must clearly cast vision, operationalize your mission, and leverage your core values as guiding principles to cultivate culture and prioritize purpose effectively. Working to get buy-in from employees on the organization's purpose is essential, and what's even more important is having employees that are "willing to assume ownership, accountability, and responsibility." (Center of Creative Leadership) Managing change is part of the foundational work needed to advance DEI in the workplace. Focus on building a team that sees themselves as responsible for the success of the organization and apply the principles mentioned in this chapter and you will be well on your way to a more diverse, equitable, and inclusive culture.

"Diversity: The art of thinking independently together."

—Malcolm Forbes

THE BUILDING BLOCKS OF BELONGING

5 STEPS TO CREATING A DIVERSE, EQUITABLE, AND INCLUSIVE CULTURE

BY ANDREW ADENIYI

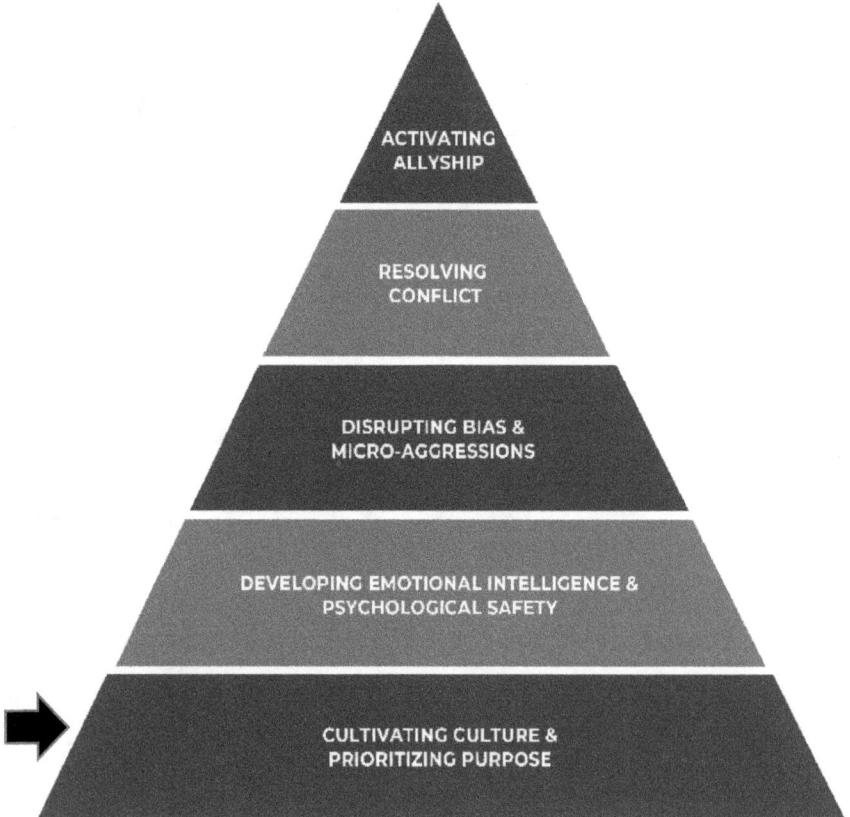

ACTIVATING ALLYSHIP

RESOLVING CONFLICT

DISRUPTING BIAS & MICRO-AGGRESSIONS

DEVELOPING EMOTIONAL INTELLIGENCE & PSYCHOLOGICAL SAFETY

CULTIVATING CULTURE & PRIORITIZING PURPOSE

www.aaasolutions.us

CHAPTER 2: INTRO TO DIVERSITY, EQUITY & INCLUSION

The second part of the first building block is about leveraging your "why" to advance and elevate DEI in the workplace. This chapter defines key terms around DEI like equality, equity, accessibility, inclusion, and more; examines the difference between equality and equity; and outlines the value of practicing DEI in the workplace.

Now that we have a basic understanding of what workplace culture is and why it matters, let's explore how DEI fits into workplace culture.

Diversity is defined as a range of human differences. It is a numerical way to categorize and classify people based on specific characteristics. Discussions on diversity often address gender, race, ethnicity, and sexual orientation. However, there are many other characteristics of diversity that are often overlooked.

Persons with disabilities (the largest minority group in the US), veterans, single parents, the formerly incarcerated, and elders are all considered underrepresented groups in the workplace. To best understand diversity, we must broaden our perspective on what it means and to whom it applies. Almost all of us are considered part of an underrepresented group when we exercise a broader application of demographic information.

One of my mentors, Jimmie McMillian, Sr. Corporate Counsel and Chief DEI officer for the Indianapolis Motor Speedway, once shared a story about the impact of diversity. Following the George Floyd murder, Jimmie was tasked with helping to create a DEI strategy for his organization. Part of that strategy included diversifying the pipeline of talent to ensure there was a diverse pool of candidates from which to select a vital HR-related intern. After selecting a Hispanic woman for the role, we'll call her Desiree, he quickly realized how valuable different perspectives are in the workplace.

One of the first suggestions Desiree provided was to have bi-lingual signage at the racetrack. With a strong population of Hispanics near the racetrack, this small but mighty idea was just the type of change Jimmie was looking for. According to **US Census Data,** 18.9% of people identify as Hispanic or Latino. So, something as simple as bi-lingual signage can help underrepresented groups feel included. And once people feel included, they are more likely to attend races which is good for business.

This is a straightforward example of how diversity of thought can benefit an organization. I always say that if there are seven of me sitting around a table making decisions about my business, I am almost certain to make substandard business decisions because I have blind spots and biases that can interfere with making the best possible decision. CEOs and senior leaders partner with subject matter experts so that the strengths of the team compensate for their individual weaknesses. This diversity of thought is where the true value of diversity lies.

In discussions about equality, the dialogue often revolves around acknowledging that women and men do not get paid equally. This gender pay gap is a serious problem because we should not have certain segments of people making less than their counterparts when they have similar experiences, backgrounds, education, etc. Disparities in pay can be demoralizing for employees and can negatively impact morale. Low morale for an extended period of time worst case will end in turnover and best case, low productivity. Equality is the state of being equal, especially in status, rights, opportunities, and race.

Equity, on the other hand, is about being fair and impartial. It is about taking a custom approach towards ensuring that all parties have what they need to be successful. Equity is strong leadership. By understanding your team well enough to know what obstacles they are facing, you can remove those obstacles and empower them to do their best work. Below is an image that illustrates the difference between equality and equity.

In the equal approach on the left, though each spectator is given the same level of assistance, only two of them are able to watch the game. In the equitable approach on the right, custom tools and resources are provided to each person (as needed) to ensure all parties can watch the game.

I once had a situation arise where a formerly employed person, let's call him Chandler, became visually impaired and wanted to return to their previous position within my client's organization. Chandler left on good terms, so I was working with the client to determine reasonable accommodations for him. We realized that Chandler needed different equipment at his workstation such as a particular monitor, unique user-friendly desk, customized keyboard and mouse to accomplish the same work that his coworker would need right next to him. You might wonder, "is that fair?" Absolutely!

Each person on your team has different needs and as their leader, it is your job to do your best to reasonably support each person. These needs may consist of not being around alcohol during company gatherings due to religious beliefs or ensuring there are inclusive food options with company provided food. Or perhaps a single father needs some wiggle room in his schedule to ensure he can pick his child up after school. If you look at equity through this lens, it will help you truly create a fair work environment for ALL, not just the groups with the loudest voices.

After graduating from college in 2013, I worked for an international retailer as a district manager. I had the belief that I needed to treat all my direct reports the same. In my mind, that was the 'fair' way to approach leading people. Although I had good intentions, I quickly realized that I could not apply an identical approach to each person on my team.

One of my managers who reported to me, we'll call her Mary, wanted information in a very direct fashion. No fluff, no positives. She wanted a list of all the problems so she could address them with clarity and certainty. If I approached one of my other managers, Michelle, the same way, she would have started crying before I could finish my notes from the visit. This is another example of how equality is not always the answer, but equity is. Taking an equitable approach towards leading your people allows you to operate under the platinum rule of treating others the way THEY want to be treated and not the way YOU think they should be treated or how you'd like for them to be treated. This example also demonstrates diversity of thought based on personality and temperament. The communication preferences between the two were very different and neither approach is right or wrong.

Now that we know equality means sameness and equity means customization, lets dive into what accessibility means. I mentioned previously that people with disabilities comprise the largest underrepresented group in America (roughly 25%). However, according to an article from The Society of Human Resource Management, 8.2% of people with a disability are unemployed compared with 3.5% as of April 2023. In addition to unconscious bias and non-inclusive hiring practices, a major reason for high levels of unemployment amongst people with disabilities is that organizations have not implemented systems to optimize equitable access to open positions.

The image below illustrates how designing systems with access in mind, saves you from problem solving on the back end. Access refers to the commitment to include everyone in all programs and activities.

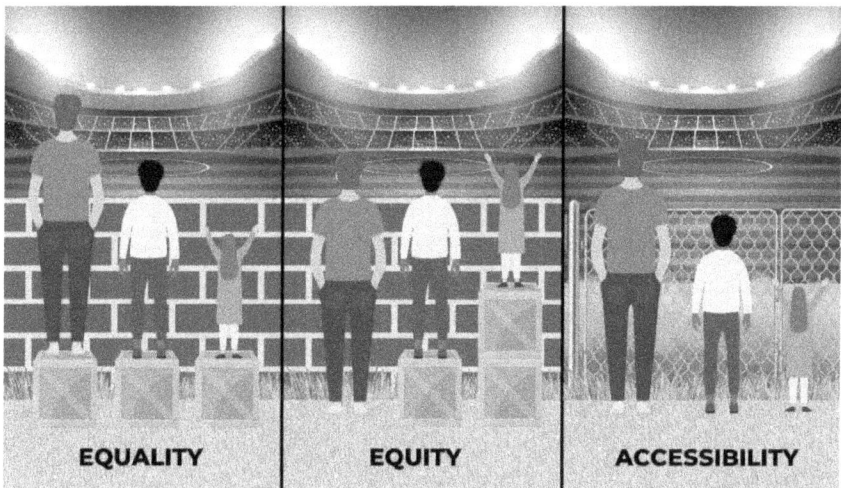

EQUALITY   EQUITY   ACCESSIBILITY

Next, let's unpack inclusion. If diversity is what makes us all unique, inclusion is how we collaboratively utilize those differences to create something more dynamic and beautiful than what could be created separately. If we think back to Jimmie's intern story, had Desiree not felt included in decision making, it is likely that she would never have suggested creating bi-lingual signage at the racetrack. This demonstrates that diversity alone is not enough. Diverse talent must feel included in the decision-making process and feel that the environment is psychologically safe enough to speak out, even if what is offered is unconventional.

We'll dive more into psychological safety later in this book, but what is most important to understand is that inclusion is a feeling of trust. Inclusion involves empowerment and respect so that people can show up as their true, authentic selves because their differences are celebrated and valued.

When you prioritize and excel in practicing DEI in an organization you foster a culture of belonging where diversity of thought is embraced and encouraged.

DEI strategist Arthur Chan says, "Diversity is a fact. Equity is a choice. Inclusion is an action. Belonging is an outcome." This is the most succinct and concise definition I have found for diversity, equity, inclusion, and belonging.

What is the connection between workplace culture and DEI? If the goal of HR is to create an engaged workforce and the goal of DEI in the workplace is to foster a culture of belonging, DEI and workplace culture are, therefore, inextricably linked. I once heard, "If you show me an employee who feels like they belong, I'll show you someone who is engaged at work. If you show me someone who is engaged at work, I'll show you someone who feels a sense of belonging." That is how DEI and workplace culture go hand in hand.

According to a study done by (Wiley), "Only 18% of workers surveyed were satisfied with their work-life balance, and workers who left a company did so because they said they **did not feel like they were valued or that they belonged.**" This statistic illustrates and quantifies the impact of a workplace culture that promotes and prioritizes it's employees' sense of belonging.

Countless studies have shown the value of diversity in the workplace.

Below are a few examples:

- "A 1% increase in gender diversity has proven to result in a minimum 3% increase in sales revenues." *(Source: Diversity Best Practices)*
- Companies with at least three women directors have experienced 66% return on capital investment, 42% increase on return on sales, and 53% increase on return on equity *(Source: Fast Company)*
- "Well-managed diverse work teams produce results that are **6 times higher** than homogeneous teams." *(Source: Diversity Best Practices)*
- "Publicly traded companies on the DiversityInc Top 50 List **outperform the S&P 500 by 29% over one year** and **80% over 10 years**, and **outperform the Dow Jones Industrial Average by 20% over one year** and **50% over 10 years**." *(Source: DiversityInc)*

If you still do not see the value of diversity in the workplace, I encourage you to consider if your beliefs are rooted in facts or feelings and if you're leveraging a growth mind-set or a fixed mind-set. Once you review the facts, listen to the stories, and position yourself to be open minded, the chances of you seeing the value of diversity at work should increase. If you are following along and feel like you have a good understanding of what DEI means and why it matters in the workplace, let's move on to how you can go about acting.

My DEI firm, AAA Solutions, (www.aaasolutions.us) guides clients through a three-phase DEI Roadmap.

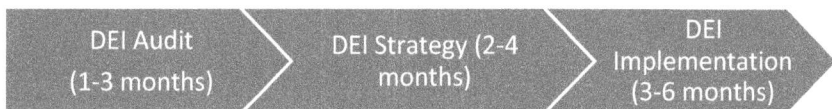

DEI Audit (1-3 months)	DEI Strategy (2-4 months)	DEI Implementation (3-6 months)

In Phase 1, the DEI Audit phase, we collect quantitative and qualitative information from clients to best understand employee sentiment around DEI related matters. This phase consists of disseminating an employee survey, reviewing all pertinent workplace culture and DEI related materials, and conducting interviews and focus group discussions.

Some of the survey questions we recommend asking your team during this phase are listed below:

- I can voice a contrary opinion without negative consequences.
- I have the same opportunities for advancement as other employees in my organization.
- I feel that my compensation is fair for the work I do.
- At work I feel comfortable being myself.
- I feel confident I can develop my career at my company.
- I feel like I belong at my company.

We always encourage using a 1-5 Likert rating scale (1=strongly disagree, 5=strongly agree) and comparing results based on various demographics. This allows you to uncover any areas of opportunities that may exist between certain underrepresented groups. This means you should collect demographic data on your DEI survey. Always articulate to your workforce why you want to collect that information and what will be done with that data. You should also include a "prefer to not disclose" option for all demographic questions.

I once had a client that did not want to include demographic questions on the survey despite my strong recommendation to do so. After a year of working with their organization on DEI related initiatives, engagement scores improved and there were some improvements regarding diversity, however we did not have a way to quantify the improvement in diversity because there was never a baseline established for various demographics.

There is a reason why scoreboards are used in sports. People need to know what the goal is and how they are performing in context of the goals in place. People need to know where the starting point is so progress can be measured. My stance on this subject aligns with the saying that "what gets measured, gets done". DEI in the workplace is no exception.

The goal of Phase 1 of the DEI Roadmap is to collect data that allows you to understand the key strengths and key opportunities that exist within your organization. This information will be vital as you move to Phase 2.

Phase 2 of the DEI Roadmap is the DEI Strategy phase. This phase is to brainstorm ways to act on the areas of opportunity that emerged from the DEI Audit phase. You want to put a plan in place to elevate and/or sustain the areas where your organization is winning. We always recommend leveraging SMART (Specific. Measurable. Attainable. Relative. Time-Sensitive.) goals so that there are metrics and due dates for each goal put in place. You should try to have a minimum of 2-3 goals and not commit to more than your organization has the bandwidth to execute.

Below are some example goals your organization could target:

- Create a cross-functional DEI committee within the next 6 months.
- Provide quarterly company-wide DEI training beginning quarter 1 of next year.
- Review all job descriptions for gender neutral and overall inclusive language before the end of the year and revise them as needed.
- Diversify your board of directors and executive leadership team to mirror the demographics of the clients you serve within the next 3 years.

The key here is to ensure your goals are in the SMART format. You also want the goals to be created based on data which helps to minimize bias in the goal-setting process. A data-driven action plan makes it easier to evaluate progress and communicate transparently.

I once had a client in the tech industry who acknowledged that DEI was important, but they did not know how to initiate sustainable positive change in their organization. After conducting a comprehensive DEI Audit and creating a data driven DEI Strategy, they hired 22 interns from underrepresented groups, improved employee engagement and the overall sense of belonging reported from the results of a pulse check survey and committed to quarterly DEI training sessions for their workforce. As a result of this work, they were nominated for a small business award in the state of Indiana for demonstrating a commitment to workplace culture and DEI.

Although the goal should not be awards and recognition, this type of acknowledgement is evidence that intentional focus on practicing DEI in the workplace has a tangible, positive impact on our organizations and the communities that we serve. This type of work attracts and retains top talent which impacts retention, productivity, and our efficiency in fulfilling our mission.

Phase 3 of the DEI Roadmap consists of DEI Implementation. In this phase of the roadmap, a diverse, cross-functional committee is formed with the purpose of executing on the SMART goals created for the organization in Phase 2. This committee will include members from all of the company's various levels and departments and reflect the demographics of the organization at large. The DEI committee also has executive level sponsorship support. This means that either the CEO or someone who reports to the CEO should be on the committee to provide executive level oversight and support.

The DEI committee ideally has two co-chairs that facilitate the meetings and handle the blocking and tackling of the committee. These tasks typically include weekly or monthly logistical and administrative tasks like scheduling meetings, brainstorming events, and sharing progress with key stakeholders. 2-year terms are recommended for each committee member to allow fresh perspectives to rotate onto the committee. Hiring an outside consultant or firm helps to drive momentum with this initiative, however with the right leadership, structure, and goals, an organization can lead this work internally.

From time to time, there may be a need to evaluate progress and get additional feedback from the larger organization to ensure the work is being felt throughout the company. In these moments, pulse check surveys can be deployed to gauge impact of the DEI Roadmap.

DEI in the workplace helps to foster a sense of belonging with your team. When people feel a sense of belonging at work, they are more engaged, and more committed to the organization. If you believe that all employees deserve to feel heard, seen, and valued at work, then you are also saying that DEI in the workplace should be prioritized. Now you must act.

"You can have courage or you can have comfort, but you cannot have both"

-Brene Brown

THE BUILDING BLOCKS OF BELONGING

5 STEPS TO CREATING A DIVERSE, EQUITABLE, AND INCLUSIVE CULTURE

BY ANDREW ADENIYI

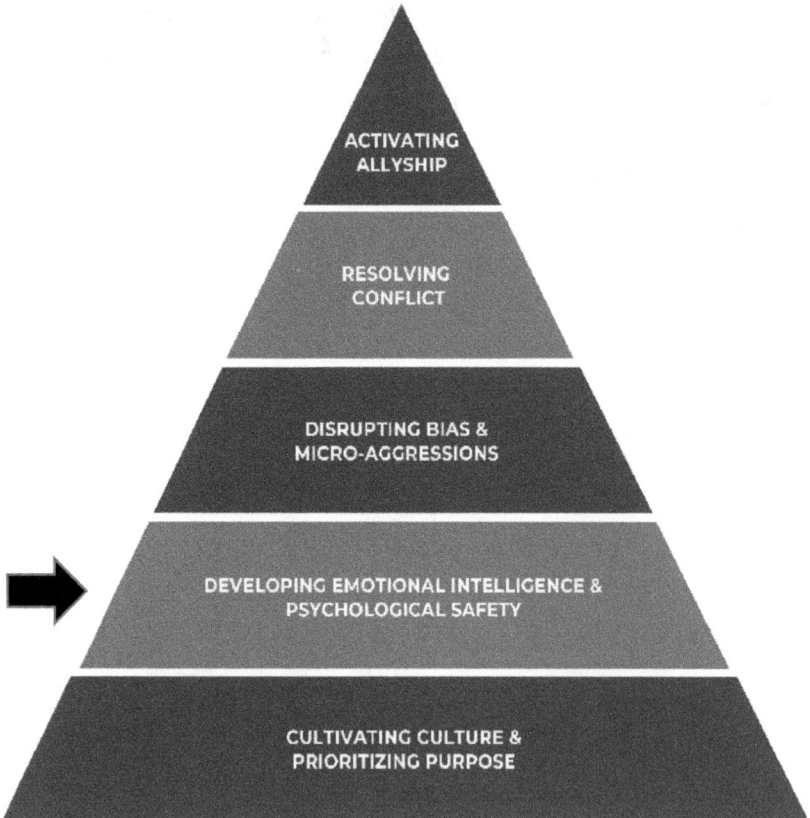

ACTIVATING ALLYSHIP

RESOLVING CONFLICT

DISRUPTING BIAS & MICRO-AGGRESSIONS

DEVELOPING EMOTIONAL INTELLIGENCE & PSYCHOLOGICAL SAFETY

CULTIVATING CULTURE & PRIORITIZING PURPOSE

www.aaasolutions.us

CHAPTER 3: DEVELOPING EMOTIONAL INTELLIGENCE (EQ) IN THE WORKPLACE

Now that we have established the foundation of The Building Blocks of Belonging, let's unpack emotional intelligence. This chapter will define emotional intelligence (EQ), discuss why it matters in the workplace, and share practical ways you can improve your EQ.

What is Emotional Intelligence?

Emotional intelligence, also known as "EQ", is the skill to recognize, understand, and manage **your emotions**, AND recognize, understand, and influence the **emotions of other people.** Think about EQ as two parts:

Part 1 = emotions of self

Part 2 = emotions of others

Both parts require awareness, understanding and the managing of emotions.

EQ Explained

EQ is not the same as IQ, intelligence quotient. IQ is rooted in intellect and is rarely improved even through tremendous effort. EQ, on the other hand, can be cultivated and focuses primarily on emotions and interpersonal relationships. We may be born with certain levels of EQ skills, but we can improve those skills by refining them. This means that practicing the components of EQ regularly will help you further develop those skill sets. When your EQ skills are refined, you're not only able to handle crucial conversations, you are able to help others do the same.

According to the Huffington Post, only **15%** of an individual's success in working effectively with others is because of technical skills, leaving **85%** to their ability to connect and have quality relationships with others. That means if you work with people, EQ is integral to your success.

Take Grace for example. Grace is a strong performer and maintains positive relationships with her peers. She exceeds the expectations of her role and provides tremendous value to the organization by consistently achieving her goals. Because Grace prides herself in her work, she does not like to procrastinate.

Michael on the other hand has been an average performer at best. He barely meets expectations and rarely goes above and beyond his role and responsibilities. With a goal of doing the minimum amount of work needed to not get fired, he does not provide nearly the amount of value to the organization as he could. Michael is not new to the team, but not yet considered a veteran at the company. He is also known to lack empathy. This became evident when he ate Rachel's lunch without asking her simply because he forgot his lunch at home and assumed Rachel would not mind. If eating his peer's lunch without their approval wasn't bad enough, he took his lack of empathy to another level when he complained about George taking off a week for his mother's funeral. Michael's inability to put himself in the shoes of some of his colleagues was putting a strain on his relationships with his peers.

In fact, some of Michael's most critical feedback has related to his difficulty in managing relationships. For example, when Grace was assigned a very demanding long-term project that the rest of the team was aware of, Michael bombarded her with questions, disrupting her focus, and flow. Michael's behavior and inability to recognize the emotional impact of his constant interruptions, caused Grace to want to limit her interactions with him.

So, if 85% of Michael's career success is contingent upon him managing relationships, the stakes are stacked against him to succeed based on how he interacted with Grace. Luckily, Grace's high EQ allowed her to quietly cooperate despite her workload increasing. Grace had every reason to be upset for Michael relying on her too much, but she self-regulated her emotions to ensure she did not allow how she felt to get the best of her. Despite being under immense stress, Grace continued to act with tact, dignity, and respect.

However, Grace also has an opportunity for growth here. If Grace developed the courage and was equipped with the tools to give Michael feedback, this issue may have been resolved sooner. Grace's heart for service and desire to be liked and respected at work led her to being slow to provide critical feedback to Michael which may have enabled Michael to continue his less than desirable behavior.

We will discuss later in this book how to effectively resolve conflict but if Grace selected a time to speak to Michael about his behavior, started positive during the conversation and clearly articulated what she's been experiencing and how that is impacting her, Michael may have gotten the wakeup call he needed to change. For example, Grace could have opened the conversation like this:

"Hey Michael, thanks for carving out time in your schedule to chat with me. I really appreciate your eagerness to learn and the amount of curiosity you bring to the team and the organization. The knowledge you can gain by asking the questions that you do, is admirable. However, I have been finding myself feeling frustrated and overwhelmed by the volume of questions you have been asking and the timing of when you ask them. When there are several questions, I must answer daily that require well thought out and detailed responses, it takes me away from other obligations I have which causes me a great deal of stress.

What I do not want is for you to feel like you cannot come to me when you have questions. I know there are still some things you do not know which is understandable. What I do want to see happen is you utilizing all your resources and training materials prior to asking questions. I also think that saving your non-time sensitive questions for a time to be sent over maybe in one email would also feel less overwhelming to me. I value our working relationship and want to see you do well so what are your thoughts on what I just shared?"

This flow of conversation is one of many ways to engage in what can be a challenging conversation. With Grace starting the conversation being positive, this will help Michael not be as defensive as he would be had she led with her issues with him. Grace also demonstrated high EQ by being clear, yet kind with communicating what she is feeling and why she is experiencing those feelings. She continued by expressing what she does not want to happen as well as clarifying what she does want to happen. If Grace transitions to being an active listener as she passes Michael the mic, she will be better able to paraphrase Michael's comments, ask follow up questions, and collaborate on a path forward.

Daniel Goleman from Harvard Business Review breaks down EQ into 5 buckets.

1. Self-Awareness

EQ begins with self-awareness. The ability to recognize and evaluate your emotional strengths and triggers. Take a moment to ask yourself, "How am I feeling?" Be specific and honest with your answer. This allows you to then do some self-discovery regarding why you are feeling that way.

2. Self-management

Self-Management is being able to slow down, think, and hold yourself accountable for decision-making. Being able to self-regulate empowers you to manage your emotions instead of letting them manage you.

3. Motivation

Motivation is about having a growth-mindset; being intentional with optimism and hope; walking with the clarity of vision that comes from understanding your why. Long-term thinking around compelling goals can help with sustaining motivation.

4. Empathy

Empathy is about curiosity and perspective-taking. Being curious and patient enough to understand someone else's perspective helps to build trust and commitment. It allows us the thrill of vulnerability and meaningful connection.

5. Conflict Resolution

To have strong social skill, you must be effective at conflict resolution. Improving your communication skills will help you become more influential to others which will help you sustain positive relationships with others. I define influence as the ability to alter someone's behavior. During a conversation, this happens from being able to understand body language as well as verbal communication and tone. As you grow your ability to influence behavior, you are more likely to influence results. In the workplace, this is how culture forms. From consistently influencing behavior and establishing expectations for how people interact.

Four quadrants of Emotional Intelligence:

The best way to grow your organization is to grow your leaders. Part of growing your leaders must include being able to get the most out of your team which requires emotional intelligence. Becoming the organization that attracts quality talent can only be accomplished through leadership and workplace culture, which both involve effective communication and cultivating relationships.

Although we have introduced the five components of EQ, I want to highlight another framework that may be helpful. According to the article titled, "Emotional Intelligence Frameworks, Charts, Diagrams, & Graphs" by Leslie Riopel, here is a four-quadrant framework that breaks down EQ into the following categories:

- Self-Awareness (Personal Competence & Recognition)

- Self-Management (Personal Competence & Regulation)

- Social Awareness (Social Competence & Recognition)

- Relationship Management (Social Competence & Regulation)

When it comes to self-awareness, the framework highlights self-confidence and awareness of your emotions as key. Self-management focuses more on self-discipline and regulation. Social awareness is observing all verbal and non-verbal social cues to distill what is and is not being said in the room. Lastly, relationship management requires clarity in communication and conflict resolution.

This is one of many frameworks out there on EQ but most, if not all of them, focus on being more empathetic with others.

	Recognition	Regulation
Personal Competence	**Self-Awareness** • Self-confidence • Awareness of your emotional state • Recognizing how your behavior impacts others • Paying attention to how others influence your emotional state	**Self-Management** • Keeping disruptive emotions and impulses in check • Acting in congruence with your values • Handling change flexibly • Pursuing goals and opportunities despite obstacles and setbacks
Social Competence	**Social Awareness** • Picking up on the mood in the room • Caring what others are going through • Hearing what the other person is "really" saying	**Relationship Management** • Getting along well with others • Handling conflict effectively • Clearly expressing ideas/information • Using sensitivity to another person's feeling (empathy) to manage interactions successfully

Sympathy vs. Empathy

Many people use sympathy and empathy interchangeably, but they have very distinct differences. If your colleague, Tyler is going through a difficult divorce, sympathetic approach might include statements like "Oh I feel so bad for you Tyler" or "Poor Tyler, that is terrible". Although they show compassion, these statements lack the deep connection and understanding present in true empathy.

An empathetic approach to that situation may include statements like "How are you feeling right now Tyler?" and "How can I best support you?" While sympathy is about feelings of compassion for someone else without genuine understanding, empathy is about imagining yourself in the same situation to connect with the emotions, beliefs, and thoughts of the other person.

Empathetic approaches are, therefore, centered around the other person and their wants and needs instead of your own. This does not mean that your feelings do not matter, however, your feelings simply should not take center stage. Empathy is about having a holistic perspective in terms of being able to see things from multiple perspectives. Empathy is inclusive of self and other which gives you a better picture and enables you to interact with more grace. You must be willing to put yourself in someone else's situation to truly demonstrate empathy. Even if you did not like Tyler's spouse and you gave advice in the past to end the marriage sooner, empathy requires you to suspend your judgement and exercise curiosity to fully understanding your colleague's feelings and perspective. This may be challenging, however, in the workplace, empathy is a rewarding practice critical to cultivating meaningful and productive partnerships.

The Emotionally Intelligent Person

The term EQ was coined by two American Psychologists, John Mayer and Peter Salovey in 1990. However, in the over 30 years since the concept of EQ was introduced, many organizations are still not effective at developing the emotional intelligence of their workforce. By intentionally developing the emotional intelligence of your team members, you are equipping them with the ability to identify, leverage, understand, and regulate emotions: all foundational elements of influence and communication.

A person shows their emotional intelligence by doing the following:

1. Active listening (Repeat back what you heard)
2. Committing to collaboration
3. Being curious
4. Asking open ended questions
5. Being aware of tone, verbal, and body language
6. Asking for feedback

The awareness of emotions can be tricky at times. Often, we do not have the vocabulary to verbalize our feelings. I have found the emotion wheel to be extremely helpful on my personal journey of understanding my emotions. If you are not familiar with the emotion wheel, I encourage you to do a quick google search to get a visual.

The emotion wheel helps you pinpoint the true emotions that you are experiencing. Although you may start out in the middle of the emotion wheel labeling your emotions as fearful or angry, going deeper and getting even more specific can land you at an emotion along the outer wheel such as exposed or skeptical.

The emotional wheel helps you navigate to the exact emotion you are feeling. Extreme outbursts of negative emotions rarely produce positive long-term outcomes so staying present with your own emotions is a healthy leadership habit. Although you may think you are simply "sad" in a situation, the emotion wheel helps you be more precise with recognizing your emotions. You may start with "sad", and by using the emotions wheel, realize that you are "embarrassed".

Perspective-Taking

Perspective taking involves reserving judgement in a social exchange and considering the feelings of the person you are communicating with. This allows you to truly understand where someone is coming from. Perspective-taking enables you to image what it would feel like to be in their position. Let's look at some thoughts around practicing perspective-taking:

Practice Perspective-Taking

- Recall a stressful incident at work.
- Visualize yourself floating above the incident like an out of body experience.
- What shifts may take place in your emotional state based on when you are in the situation vs. above the situation?
- Where do you see an opportunity for improvement of your recognition and management of yours and others emotions?
- How would practicing perspective-taking help you at work?

Inspiration for content:

YouTube Video: Leading with Emotional Intelligence in the Workplace, Carolyn Stern

YouTube Video: Daniel Goleman Introduces Emotional Intelligence, Big Think

Greek philosopher Epicitus' saying, "We have two ears and one mouth so we can listen twice as much as we speak," offers insight on perspective-taking. You cannot put yourself in someone's shoes without actively listening and asking open ended questions with a genuine sense of curiosity.

Let's look at this workplace example provided by Positive Psychology:

> "Jane works at an advertising agency, and things can get a little hectic during the brainstorming process. Everyone struggles to get their opinion heard, thinking they have the best idea. Quite often, this leads to a lot of raised voices. When…Bob presents a campaign idea, it's difficult for him to get his point across without another team member talking over him, which demonstrates very little respect and can lead to hurt feelings.
>
> Before the next meeting, Jane calmly suggests that people listen quietly to one another when others are presenting. With this simple request, Jane is demonstrating strong emotional intelligence. Specifically, she's perceiving that Bob is feeling disrespected and she's attempting to manage emotions in the room. Both recognition and effective handling of the team's emotions are at play.
>
> When everyone starts to listen to one another, per Jane's suggestion, it's much simpler to reach a constructive decision together."

This example showcases how you can interject and advocate in situations where you sense emotions being overlooked or elevating. By Jane putting herself in Bob's shoes and listening to what is and is not being said by Bob, she can be intentional with finding adequate solutions. Jane can also take this a step further and empower Bob to speak for himself by role playing him advocating for himself or providing feedback that can help him avoid shutting down in the future.

Having the motivation to practice empathy is easier when you understand the benefits. From higher productivity to less turnover, teams that work well together and foster psychological safety (will discuss in next chapter), perform much higher than teams that are not cohesive and not safe for interpersonal risk-taking. Psychological safety helps teams feel safe going against the grain and provide critical feedback that may not be popular. This interpersonal risk-taking is challenging without self-awareness and social skill. High levels of EQ enable you to better challenge the status quo and maintain psychological safety in the workplace. That is how practicing empathy can contribute to psychological safety.

Empathy

Empathy is the most important aspect of EQ. If you do not take into consideration the ideas, feelings, and thoughts of the person you are talking to, you are essentially having a monologue and not a dialogue. An exchange of information must occur for a conversation to take place so try to listen more than you speak and grow at asking better questions. According to the article titled, "The Young and the Clueless", by Bunker, Kram, and Ting, "Research has shown that the higher a manager rises in the ranks, the more important soft leadership skills are to his success." Empathy certainly applies to soft leadership skills.

In an article in *Harvard Business Review* titled "Making Empathy Central to Your Company Culture", the author states that "Research shows that empathic workplaces tend to enjoy stronger collaboration, less stress, and greater morale, and their employees bounce back more quickly from difficult moments such as layoffs." Investing in the emotional intelligence of your employees will tangibly improve empathy. Even though empathy would be considered a "soft skill", I believe empathy can serve as a competitive advantage.

The article goes on to share 3 ways to develop EQ:

1. **Have a growth mindset over a fixed mindset.** This state of mind will help you value continuous improvement and personal development.

2. **Recognize the correct norms.** Chances are there are examples of people being empathetic in your workplace right now. They key is to acknowledge them and celebrate them to positively reinforce that behavior.

3. **Leadership is key.** Just like everything else, improving the EQ of your team requires effective leadership. This means that leaders must commit to collaborating and co-creating with the team to create custom solutions for growing empathy. From performance reviews to one-on-one meetings with direct reports, leaders must be intentional with exemplifying empathy in the workplace and amplifying its importance.

Another article from The Center for Creative Leadership, titled "The Importance of Empathy in the Workplace", breaks down how empathy is a vital leadership competency. According to the article, "empathy in the workplace is positively related to job performance... managers who practiced empathetic leadership toward direct reports were viewed as better performers by their bosses... those managers who were rated as empathetic by subordinates were also rated as high performing by their own boss."

This research illustrates the correlation between a "soft skill" like empathy and bottom-line results (performance). If you work with people, empathy should be important to you. If it has not yet been a priority, I hope this serves as your call to action to change that.

Developing your EQ

Let's assume you are ready to develop your EQ. Here are 3 things you can begin working on today:

1. **Self-reflection** – Take time to practice mindfulness and getting to know your strengths and weaknesses. This can be done through a personal **SWOT analysis and/**or through soliciting feedback from peers. This work helps you to **uncover personal blind spots** that otherwise would have been left uncovered. Blind spots are areas you do not have clear visibility and understanding of. Understanding your triggers and exploring why they trigger you is also a part of self-reflection.

    - Ex. Knowing strict deadlines cause you to be short and quick tempered with others so you become intentional with setting realistic goals to give yourself adequate time to work on projects. This type of realistic self-assessment improves trustworthiness and integrity.

2. **Empathize with others** – Be willing to see things from a different perspective. By trying to perceive situations from the perspective of others, you will foster a stronger connection which improves trust through vulnerability and compassion. Practice **active listening** and asking open-ended questions to gather information. Be curious and pay attention to non-verbal communication to find out more about how someone is truly reacting to a situation.

    - Ex: After your VP of Sales has produced three consecutive quarters of decreased performance, you try to understand how they are feeling and why.

Throughout the discovery process you learn about the terminal illness of their father. This helps you ask the right questions and position yourself as a supportive leader rather than an insensitive boss. Being clear is kind so it is also important to align on expectations to ensure overall performance improves.

3. **Hold yourself accountable** – Take responsibility of your emotional reactions. Work diligently at performing at a higher social level by asking for feedback and acting on the feedback you receive.

   - Ex. When Alex is not prepared for a board meeting, it reflects poorly on you as his manager. Instead of resorting to yelling and scolding Alex, you ask open ended questions to see what you could have done to better prepare him. Collaborating on solutions while being clear on expectations moving forward is a way of practicing empathetic leadership.

EQ & DEI in the Workplace

So, what is the connection between EQ and DEI? As discussed earlier, DEI is about celebrating diversity of thought and fostering a culture of belonging. When you empathize with people and show genuine interest in how someone is feeling, this is practicing emotional intelligence which will lead to a stronger sense of belonging. I believe EQ is a differentiator between good and exceptional leaders. Therefore, EQ is a fundamental ingredient for thriving diverse, equitable, and inclusive cultures.

According to "What Makes a Leader" by Daniel Goleman in Harvard Business Review on EQ, empathy is about understanding other people's emotional makeup and that makeup is largely influenced by their lived experiences, beliefs, identity, etc. which is what diversity essentially is. According to Goleman, some of the hallmarks of an empathetic leader include:

- Expertise in attracting and retaining talent
- Ability to develop others
- Sensitivity to cross-cultural differences

Goleman goes on to give an example of an American consultant and her team. The team pitches a project to a prospective client in Japan. Her team interprets the client's silence as disapproval and prepares to leave. The consultant reads the client's body language and senses interest. She continues the meeting, and her team gets the job. This is a very simplified example; however, the value of understanding emotions is critical for building and maintaining relationships. The more diverse your organization, empathy and EQ increase in importance.

Emotional capabilities help you influence people from a place of influence and respect rather coercion or manipulation. When you can influence behavior, you are able to impact results and that is what EQ allows you to tap into. EQ is important when it comes to change management as well as creating and leading teams. Change management is all about applying a structured approach towards altering the status quo. Since changing behavior requires managing emotions, EQ plays a big role in achieving a desired outcomes relating to change management principles.

Imagine you learned through 360-degree performance review feedback that empathy is one of your weaknesses as a leader. Framing this new information as an opportunity will help motivate you to focus on growth. You can leverage a mentor or a coach to work with you on improving or use a trusted friend or colleague to role play and talk through some scenarios. With EQ, practice makes perfect. Feedback is valuable, so get comfortable with the uncomfortable, and understand that your decision as a leader to develop your EQ plays a significant role in creating belonging and trust in the workplace.

According to Goleman,

"Emotional intelligence is born largely in the neurotransmitters of the brain's limbic system, which governs feelings, impulses, and drives. Research indicates that the limbic system learns best through motivation, extended practice, and feedback.

Compare this with the kind of learning that goes on in the neocortex, which governs analytical and technical ability. The neocortex grasps concepts and logic. It is the part of the brain that figures out how to use a computer or make a sales call by reading a book."

Goleman's article goes on to mention David McClelland (renowned researcher in human and organizational behavior) and his 1996 study of "...a global food and beverage company. McClelland found that when senior managers had a critical mass of emotional intelligence capabilities, their divisions outperformed yearly earnings goals by 20%. Meanwhile, division leaders without that critical mass underperformed by almost the same amount."

According to the article titled, "Primal Leadership", by Goleman, Boyatzis, and McKee:

1. "High levels of emotional intelligence, our research showed, create climates in which information sharing, trust, healthy risk-taking, and learning flourish. Low levels of emotional intelligence create climates rife with fear and anxiety."
2. "If a leader's mood and accompanying behaviors are indeed such potent drivers of business success, then a leader's premier task-we would even say his primal task-is emotional leadership."
3. "Research shows that a leader's emotional style also drives everyone else's moods and behaviors - through a neurological process called mood contagion ('smile and the whole world smiles with you.')"

By thinking about where you are today in your leadership capabilities and where you ultimately want to be, you can start casting vision for a more developed you. Willingness to put yourself in new situations and experiences is mandatory for maximizing your EQ. This could be as simple as taking on a volunteer opportunity or a leadership position in your church. Diverse social settings make you flex muscles you may not have known existed. This process of intentional exposure can be very informative and rewarding.

EQ in Groups

According to "Building the Emotional Intelligence of Groups" by Vanessa Urch Druskat and Steven B. Wolf, "three conditions are essential to a group's effectiveness: trust among members, a sense of group identity, and a sense of group efficacy." This research reveals that trust, and a shared sense of purpose are critical for group success. This is why understanding others in the workplace is important for developing high functional teams.

The article discusses how "emotionally intelligent norms" can reinforce a culture of high EQ. These norms are simply "attitudes and behaviors that eventually become habits". The healthy habits you adopt can increase your emotional capacity which is "the ability to respond constructively in emotionally uncomfortable situations". When you create an affirmative environment and reward collaborative problem solving, you are setting yourself and your team up for success.

The article goes on to state "Group emotional intelligence is about the small acts that make a big difference. It is not about a team member working all night to meet a deadline; it is about saying thank you for doing so. It is not about in-depth discussion of ideas; it is about asking a quiet member for his thoughts. It is not about harmony, lack of tension, and all members liking each other; it is about acknowledging when harming is false, tension is unexpressed, and treating others with respect."

The ramifications of a team member who severely lacks EQ can be catastrophic. According to "The Price of Incivility" BY Porath & Pearson, "Just one habitually offensive employee critically positioned in your organization can cost you dearly in lost employees, lost customers, and lost productivity". Having someone who consistently rubs people the wrong way can cost you proportionately to the amount of influence and authority that individual has.

According to "Emotional Agility" by Susan David and Christina Congleton,

"Emotional agility enables people to approach their inner experiences in a mindful, values-driven, and productive way rather than buying into it trying to surprise them." To aid in this process, below are four practices adapted from Acceptance and Commitment Therapy (ACT):

1. Recognize your patterns
2. Label your thoughts and emotions
3. Accept them
4. Act on your values

In conclusion, EQ is all about recognizing, understanding, and managing emotions in yourself and others. We know that EQ can be developed so once we understand what it is and why it matters, we must be accountable and take action. Intentionality with managing interpersonal relationships in the workplace could be the differentiator in your professional success. Regardless of if you use a journal for reflection, a podcast for knowledge, or a mentor for coaching, you must take action to develop your EQ.

> *"**Social skill is friendliness with a purpose**: moving people in the direction you desire."*
>
> -Daniel Goleman

THE BUILDING BLOCKS OF BELONGING

5 STEPS TO CREATING A DIVERSE, EQUITABLE, AND INCLUSIVE CULTURE

BY ANDREW ADENIYI

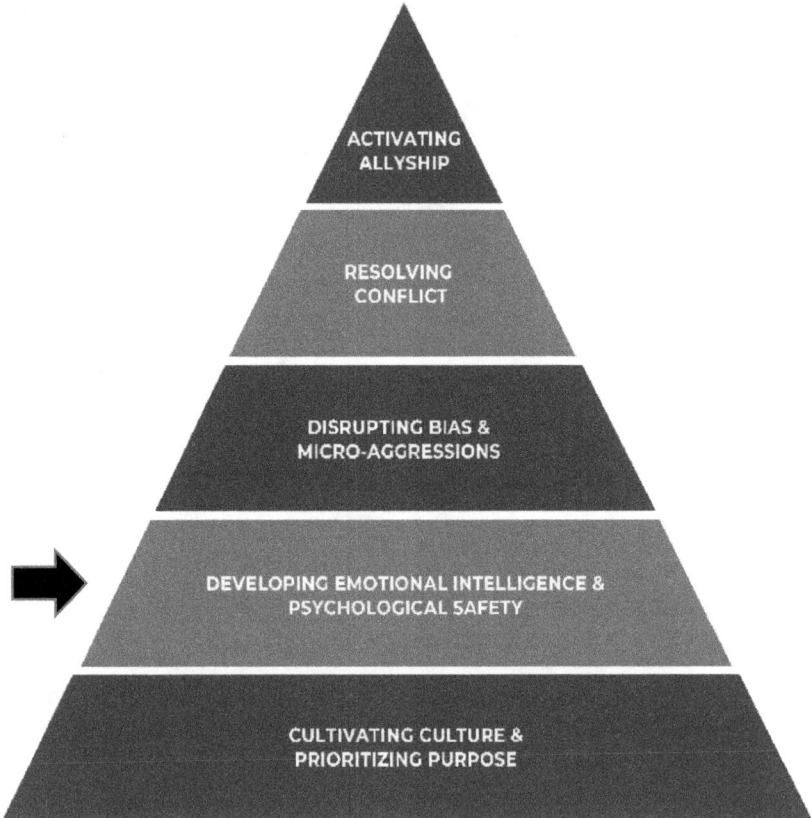

ACTIVATING ALLYSHIP

RESOLVING CONFLICT

DISRUPTING BIAS & MICRO-AGGRESSIONS

DEVELOPING EMOTIONAL INTELLIGENCE & PSYCHOLOGICAL SAFETY

CULTIVATING CULTURE & PRIORITIZING PURPOSE

www.aaasolutions.us

"Psychological safety is about candor and willingness to engage in productive conflict so as to learn from different points of view."

-Amy Edmondson

CHAPTER 4: FOSTERING PSYCHOLOGICAL SAFETY

This second component of the second building block will unpack psychological safety. This chapter covers content that will help with self-awareness, managing relationships, and fostering an environment of trust, vulnerability, and innovation.

Lack of Psychological Safety

At this point we have discussed the purpose of DEI at work and how healthy organizations encourage diversity of thought and sustain a culture of belonging. We have discussed the keys to develop emotional intelligence and now we will turn our attention towards fostering psychological safety in the workplace. However, before we define what, psychological safety is, why it matters and how to improve it, let's start with a story that speaks to what happens when psychological safety is not present.

Jameka was hesitant to speak up during a monthly meeting with the Executive Leadership Team (ELT) at her company. Although her unique background and experience could provide a ton of value given the nature of the strategic initiative the group was discussing, she could tell that her opinion would not only go against the group, but it would also go against the CEO's preference who she reported to.

To make the situation even more challenging, Jameka was still relatively new to the organization, was one of 2 women out of 8 leaders on the ELT and was the only person of color on the team. Furthermore, as the COO of the organization, Jameka was responsible for the operations which is the function of the business the strategic initiative would impact least.

Jameka was quickly weighing the pros and cons of her options in her head until she remembered the values of the organization: honesty, accountability, teamwork, and achieving results. Suddenly the answer became clear that she was going to go against the grain and voice her unpopular opinion. In the spirit of being honest and doing her part to ensure the organization achieves results, she figured it was the right thing to do.

As the CEO (we'll call him Jim) stated to the ELT, "Alright, are there any other thoughts or ideas anyone wants to share?", Jameka gathered up the courage to state, "I know you all are passionate about this initiative, however, I think the overall direction you all are leaning towards is not going to work." She then went on to explain how her previous employer made a similar decision and the ELT there regretted it and even shared another solution the team should consider.

To her disappointment, she could tell that her opinion was not well received. The rest of the ELT stopped making eye contact with her as they either looked down at their laptops or looked at Jim to gauge his reaction. Jim then looked at Jameka and told her that she was not tenured enough to know the best course of action and the company would not be adopting her recommendation. As he quickly began to move onto the next agenda item, Jameka wanted to crawl under the table and hide for the rest of the meeting. She felt embarrassed, disregarded, and angry that her viewpoint was shot down so abruptly.

Unfortunately, there are people across the world who are experiencing, have experienced, or will experience a situation like Jameka's. Although Jim did not fully understand this until later, his actions had caused Jameka to feel excluded, not valued, and not safe to take interpersonal risks in the workplace. Those are the exact opposite outcomes of a psychologically safe work environment.

Imagine if Jim gave each member of the ELT advanced notice of the topic they would be discussing. Instead of asking a general question of what other ideas and thoughts the group had, he could have specifically asked Jameka for her thoughts. A personal invitation would have demonstrated that Jameka's opinions are valued. Jim could have stayed more neutral regarding his preferences around the initiative to ensure he did not sway his ELT from giving objective input.

How do you think Jameka would have felt if Jim responded to Jameka's recommendations by saying "Thank you so much for being vulnerable and bringing up some very valid challenges regarding the direction we are leaning. I would like to unpack that more to ensure I fully understand where you are coming from. Can you please tell us more?" My guess is, Jameka would have felt seen, heard, and valued. She would have been able to fully articulate why she believed her recommendation was a better option at least knowing the ELT was going to listen to her.

It is important to clarify that psychological safety does not mean that you have to adopt all the ideas that your team suggests. However, psychological safety in the workplace does mean that there will not be humiliation or punishment for anyone speaking up with ideas, questions, concerns, or failures. When psychological safety is low in an organization, it leads to turnover, low satisfaction, and poor morale.

According to an article by Culture Amp titled, "Company Culture 101", "A Columbia University study found that the likelihood of turnover at organizations where employees feel high satisfaction with company culture is 13.9%, compared to 48.4% at companies with low satisfaction."

4 Stages of Psychological Safety

According to Dr. Timothy Clark, author of *The 4 Stages of Psychological Safety*, there are 4 stages of psychological safety.

1. Inclusion Safety: This stage is all about establishing connection and a sense of belonging.
2. Learner Safety: This stage focuses on ensuring the work environment is safe for learning.
3. Contributor Safety: This stage pertains to feeling safe enough to contribute in a meaningful way.
4. Challenger Safety: This stage is all about embracing healthy conflict and a willingness to challenge the status quo for the sake of the organization.

The likelihood of Jameka or any other member of the ELT fully embracing Challenger Safety would be very low because they saw that culturally, that level of vulnerability is not rewarded. In fact, Jim sent a message loud and clear that challenging the status quo is not encouraged, subsequently putting a cap on how much psychological safety can be present in the organization and certainly on the ELT. The goal is creating an environment where you hire great people, train them well, and empower them to not only contribute in a meaningful way, but seek out positive change opportunities (Stage 4: Challenger Safety).

Here are some additional reasons why psychological safety matters:

- Improves innovation and employee engagement
- Fosters a culture of belonging
- Helps to attract and retain talent
- Mitigates legal and ethical issues

Had Jameka's attempt to contribute gone well, that would have signaled to the ELT that it is okay to innovate, and it is okay to add value even if your opinion is unpopular. This sense of safety would likely lead to more engagement during meetings for the ELT which would increase productivity. Now that we know what psychological safety is and why it matters, let's explore the relationship between DEI and psychological safety.

Psychological Safety & DEI

We know that great cultures sustain high levels of engagement, and we also know that diverse, equitable, and inclusive cultures foster a sense of belonging. So, if you want a highly engaged employee, chances are they must feel a sense of belonging in the workplace. And as our story just demonstrated, psychological safety is critical for both belonging and engagement. All these concepts intersect with each other when done well. Show me an environment where the team feels safe to take interpersonal risks and I will show you a group of people who are productive and satisfied at work.

Leaders must be careful to not bring in diverse individuals only to stifle their diverse perspectives once onboarded. Not having psychological safety in the workplace is a cancer to DEI in the workplace. On the flip side, when a culture has high levels of psychological safety, it becomes easier to leverage diversity of thought. It becomes easier to ensure systems, processes and procedures are fair and consistent. It also becomes easier to practice inclusive leadership where there is intentionality with ensuring all voices are heard and all people are respected.

I once worked with a client in the Financial Services industry and their DEI Committee was trying to determine what content to put on their marketing materials that they would take with them to a career fair at a Historically Black College & University (HBCU). One of the committee members mentioned that they should put the majors they were recruiting for on the materials. Another member suggested they list the grade levels they were recruiting for. Several other people weighed in and just as the group was starting to come to a consensus, Amber spoke up and stated, "Perhaps we should simply list the skills we would like the students to have." Amber went on to mention that she used to work in college admissions for a local university and from her experience, listing the skills needed was a more inclusive way to cast a larger net for potential candidates.

Fast forward and this client attended the HBCU career fair with a list of skills posted on their collateral. My client left that career fair with several qualified candidates from underrepresented groups. Imagine if my client had not hired Amber due to her unconventional background? There would not have been a diverse perspective shared on this topic which could have excluded possible candidates from applying. By questioning current practices, your team can begin to ask why. Why have we done it that way? Why do they need to be a Finance major? This line of thinking allows you to poke holes in traditions that may not suit you and your organization anymore.

Another take away from this story with Amber is the psychological safety she was experiencing that enabled her to voice a contrary belief. Amber felt compelled to share because the DEI co-chair (Marc) for the committee empowered his team to provide feedback and be transparent as much as possible. He led by example and had no problem being vulnerable and admitting mistakes. Marc's intentionality with ensuring the culture of his team was safe helped him get closer to accomplishing the strategic goals for the committee.

Project Aristotle

One fascinating thing about psychological safety is that is has been proven to be more important in determining success on a team than anything else. This includes things like education, experience, intellect, and comradery. In 2014 Google was amid trying to figure out how to build the best team. The initiative went on to be known as "Project Aristotle". They initially guessed that a good mix of friends or personality styles would be the key to assembling the best team. However, Google was unable to find any correlation between team membership and team success. Once they switched their focus from who was on the team to how teams interacted, they were able to make some intriguing insights.

Here are the two main findings they discovered to be key when it comes to success of a group:

1. **Equality in conversational turn-taking**
   - This is where all team members speak roughly the same amount during meetings.
2. **Ostentatious Listening**
   - This means active listening and repeating back what you hear others say.

According to Charles Duhigg, journalist and author of "Smarter Faster Better", those two items lead to psychological safety which is the "single greatest correlate with a group's success". Some of the other behaviors that Google found to be important with effective teams were dependability, structure and clarity, purpose, and impact. The key take-away here is that psychological safety is vital when it comes to workplace culture, DEI, teamwork, and overall group success.

Charles Duhigg published an article in the New York Times Magazine in February 2016, discussing the project and he went on to mention how researchers from the people analytics team reviewed academic literature on team effectiveness which was led by Julia Rozovsky. Things such as "educational backgrounds, hobbies, friends, personality traits and more" were evaluated in "180 teams from all over the company." They found that high engaged and high intellect individuals needed psychological safety in the workplace to perform at their highest levels.

Unfortunately, there are countless statistics that indicate there are not high enough levels of psychological safety in workplaces across the world. According to Gallup, 3 out of 10 employees strongly agreed that their opinions don't count at work. A recent survey from Catalyst found that nearly half of female business leaders face difficulties speaking up in virtual meetings, and 1 in 5 reported feeling overlooked or ignored during video meetings. The truth is that without intentionality around rewarding vulnerability, team members will not feel safe to challenge assumptions and contribute in innovative ways.

Self-assessment

I encourage you to reflect on the current level of psychological safety in your workplace. Here are some questions to ponder:

- When was the last time someone challenged the status quo during a meeting?
- How did you and others respond to that situation?
- How often will someone on your team feel comfortable enough to say "I don't know" when they are asked a question, they think they should be able to answer.
- Do you encourage your team to share constructive criticism?
- Does your leader regularly ask for feedback?

Although you are beginning your psychological safety journey with education and self-reflecting, my hope is that you do not stop there. Let's talk through ways to create psychological safety in the workplace.

Five Ways to Help Create Psychological Safety

According to The Center for Creative Leadership, there are 5 ways to help create psychological safety:

1. Make it a priority
    a. There is power in explicitly stating that psychological safety is important. When the leadership in an organization backs up statements like that by leading by example, prioritizing psychological safety can be transformational for a workplace.
    b. Over-communicate the desire for creating a psychologically safe work environment before meetings, during townhalls, and other situations where leaders are communicating to their teams.

2. Facilitate everyone speaking up
    a. People should not have to mentally choose between remaining silent vs. sharing what could be valuable information simply because of how others may respond.
    b. You'll never reap the benefits of diverse viewpoints if people do not feel comfortable going against the grain and voicing unconventional ideas and thoughts.
3. Establish norms for how failure is handled
    a. Embrace a failing forward philosophy where failures within the areas of responsibility of each team member is normalized. We are not talking about catastrophic failures that put your organization at risk of going out of business, but we are talking about pushing boundaries and feeling empowered to try new things within reason.
    b. Creating a culture where failures are shared and celebrated can incentive a team to be more innovative.
4. Create space for new ideas
    a. Fear stifles creativity so if you are in a knowledge intensive environment where collaboration is high, you want to minimize the level of fear your team experiences in the workplace.
    b. You never know what ideas will ignite an exceptional thought that would have otherwise been dormant.
5. Embrace productive conflict
    a. People often think that conflict is bad. That is incorrect. Unhealthy conflict is bad; however, healthy conflict is common within the most engaged teams. When you have healthy conflict, you are productively debating ideas and strategies while respecting the person(s) you are communicating with.

    b. The most impactful knowledge sharing can happen amid heated debate as long as all parties have established trust and are actively listening.

Let's examine how Cerwin, who is the Director of Data Analytics for a boutique consulting firm handled creating more psychological safety in the workplace. After learning about the power of psychological safety and reflecting on moments in his career where that was not present, Cerwin was determined to elevate the level of psychological safety on his team. After reviewing the 5 steps mentioned earlier, he decided to do the following:

1. Establish ground rules prior to each team meeting where he voiced how much he wanted to create an open and honest environment where everyone felt psychologically safe. He was committed to publicly highlighting team members who displayed vulnerability and courage with challenging the status quo.

2. Prior to each meeting, Cerwin would send out the agenda and meet individually with people on his team he thought may be slow to share their thoughts during the meeting. He encouraged them to speak up and shared how much he values their input during team meetings. If he noticed that some folks on his team have not shared their opinion in a while, he committed to asking them to weigh in on agenda items to ensure their voice is heard.

3. Cerwin began instituting "Fail Forward Fridays" where everyone on the team would share one "failure" they had from the week as well as what they learned from the experience. Cerwin would go first each week and share candidly where he fell short and how he planned to avoid that failure moving forward. This provided a safe environment for other team members to share as well.

4. Each week, Cerwin would end his team meetings with gratitude. During the gratitude portion of the agenda, he would

recognize a team member who contributed in a meaningful way by sharing an innovative idea, failing forward, and/or being vulnerable. This behavior helped to normalize sharing new ideas, even ones that were not well thought out.

5. Cerwin leveraged a few go-to questions to encourage productive conflict. He was intentional with playing "devil's advocate" prior to making any final decisions by asking questions like, "What could go wrong with this decision?" and "What have we not considered that could be a barrier for success with this topic?" By creating time to discuss alternative views, this gave team members an invitation to debate and share contrary views to what had already been discussed.

With intentionality, courage, and asking insightful questions, you can begin creating more psychological safety in your workplace as well, just like Cerwin. Let's now turn our attention towards what the end result can look like when we create a fearless organization.

The Fearless Organization

The Fearless Organization is a book about creating psychological safety in the workplace. The book was written by Amy C. Edmondson from the Harvard Business School, and it unpacks how to create a culture of continuous improvement, innovation, and growth. In the book, Amy mentions how "Fear inhibits learning. Research in neuroscience shows that fear consumes physiologic resources, diverting them from parts of the brain that manage working memory and process new information. This impairs analytic thinking, creative insight, and problem solving."

Acknowledging the negative implications of fear in the workplace helps to set the stage for how to get your team to not withhold ideas and thoughts for improvement. Leaders must make it okay for team members to remain in dialogue. Meaning that conversation should continuously flow up until the point of a decision being made. When there is silence during discussion, leaders must ensure that conversation is not being stifled due to the perceived safety that comes with being quiet. Reading body language and asking generating insight questions can help to get people to talk.

Amy goes on to state that, "Research also shows a relationship between psychological safety and innovation. For instance, Chi-Cheng Huang and Pin-Chen Jiang collected survey data from 245 members of 60 Research and Development (R&D) teams in several Taiwanese technology firms and found that psychologically safe teams outperformed others." Employees are able to engage in meaningful ways when they are not using mental and emotional energy to calculate if a situation is safe for them to weigh in.

Amy also mentions the connection between diversity and psychological safety in the book by referencing the following research: "One recent study showed that psychological safety can make or break achievement of team performance in diverse teams. The researchers surveyed master's students participating in 195 teams in a French university and found that expertise-diverse teams performed well when psychological safety was high and badly otherwise." When people have diverse perspectives, it takes courage to challenge other people in the group who are just as smart and experienced as you are. Sometimes, the people you may be challenging are even more experienced and knowledgeable than you.

However, regardless of the tenure differences or IQ profiles of the members of the team, cultures that value diversity of thought are often best positioned to extract the knowledge and expertise from all team members. According to Amy, "In one study in a Midwestern mid-size manufacturing company, a positive climate for diversity and psychological safety together led to more discretionary effort. These relationships were stronger for minorities than for whites, suggesting that psychological safety may be playing an especially crucial role for minorities in creating engagement and a feeling of being valued at work."

When you are one of the only people that look like you on a team, it can be especially difficult to challenge the status quo. That is why as your team gets more diverse, creating a psychologically safe work environment becomes even more critical. Below are some questions to ask yourself when evaluating how fearless of environment you have at your organization:

- How often do team members speak truth to power in your organization?
- How do team members handle sharing less than desirable news up the chain of command?
- Does the organization have excessive confidence in the leadership team?
- How often do team members admit they do not know the answer to something?

The answers to those questions should help you start to evaluate if your organization or team is at risk of a potential business failure due to lack of psychological safety in the workplace. As Amy states in her book, "Early information about shortcomings can nearly always mitigate the size and impact of future, large scale failure." Fearless organizations are committed to failing forward, innovating, and managing and resolving conflict in the workplace.

Avoidable Failure

February 1, 2003, is a date that NASA and many Americans will never forget. This was the day where a potential avoidable failure was not prevented due to a lack of psychological safety. NASA's Space Shuttle Columbia unfortunately disintegrated upon reentry during a launch on that fateful day, killing everyone on board. To make matters work, NASA Engineer Rodney Rocha had voiced a concern to his supervisor a few weeks prior after watching footage on a previous launch. Rodney saw something strange dislodge from the space shuttle after taking flight but could not clearly see what it was.

After requesting additional support to obtain satellite images to better see some debris that appeared to fall off the space shuttle, his request was denied. This request would have required several levels up the chain of command to get involved in order to approve the access to the satellite images. For whatever reason, Rodney's leader was not willing to initiate the unusual request to his superiors.

During the final formal mission management team meeting before the launch, Rodney did not speak up and share his concerns with the larger group. According to Amy's book, after the Space Shuttle Columbia incident, when Rodney was asked about why he did not speak up, he said the following:

["I just couldn't do it. I'm too low down [in the organization] …and she [meaning Mission Management Team Leader Linda Ham] is way up here," gesturing with his hand held above his head.]

We'll never know if the images would have definitively helped avoid the catastrophic failure, but we do know that a lack of psychological safety prevented that option from even being attempted. Although an extreme example, not creating an environment where your team can challenge the status quo can literally be the difference between life and death.

Image an inexperienced, yet fully trained, nurse observing a doctor getting ready to perform on the wrong foot of a patient. Fear and doubt may make him question if he should really tell the doctor she is about to make a huge mistake. In some instances, nurses may second guess themselves just assuming the doctor knows what they are doing. Other situations may unfold where the nurse does inform the doctor of their pending mistake, only to get scolded for questioning his ability to do his job. The point is, all leaders must be intentional with ensuring their team feels comfortable sharing information regardless of if it goes against the grain or not.

Humility & Curiosity

So far, we have covered a lot. We have explored avoidable failures, cultures of psychological safety and those without it. We have seen some courageous improvement in the area through examples like Cerwin and his team. As we begin to land this plane, remember to pause and reflect in moments where you are considering withholding information in the workplace. Compare and contrast the short term vs. long term implications of remaining silent.

Below are 4 practical ways you can begin to apply this information:

1. **Prioritize Purpose:** Ensure everyone on your team knows why psychological safety is important by discussing it in an upcoming meeting.

2. **Be Curious:** Ask probing questions and play "devil's advocate" prior to making important decisions.

3. **Be Vulnerable:** Demonstrate to your team that there is power in vulnerability, trust in humility, and that courage will be rewarded and acknowledged.

4. **Encourage Failing Forward:** Prioritize continuous learning, set clear expectations, and hold people accountable while being empathetic.

By blending a growth mindset, humility, and curiosity together, you can strengthen relationships by building trust. Acknowledging that you do not have all the answers can be liberating to your team. Try to find those types of moments so you can demonstrate the behaviors you would like your team to replicate. Your team will applaud you for your confidence and willingness to share your shortcomings.

In conclusion, be an inclusive leader, an active listener, an expert facilitator, and a humble coach. This combination of skills will produce a workplace culture where people seek out the opinions of others proactively due to the belief that failure leads to success. Good luck elevating the level of psychological safety in your organization. You'll be sure to see diversity of thought better leveraged in the workplace as a result. As Amy went on to mention in her book, "Anyone can help create psychological safety. All you have to do is ask a good question with genuine curiosity or by a desire to give someone a voice."

"A culture first company is one that builds trust through vulnerability and actively seeks out employee feedback. We foster diversity and inclusion because it's reflective of the world we want to live in. When making decisions, a Culture First company always considers the impact on people and culture. Rather than seeking perfection, we place value on continuous improvement of both the culture and the individual."

-Didier Elzinga
CEO of Culture Amp

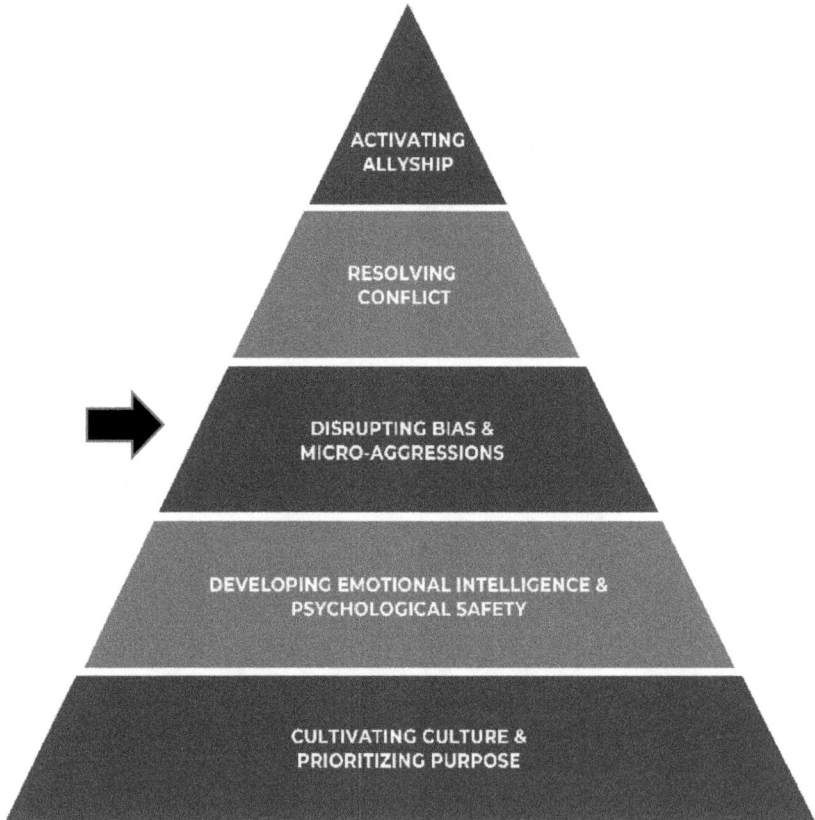

THE BUILDING BLOCKS
OF BELONGING

5 STEPS TO CREATING A DIVERSE, EQUITABLE,
AND INCLUSIVE CULTURE

BY ANDREW ADENIYI

ACTIVATING
ALLYSHIP

RESOLVING
CONFLICT

DISRUPTING BIAS &
MICRO-AGGRESSIONS

DEVELOPING EMOTIONAL INTELLIGENCE &
PSYCHOLOGICAL SAFETY

CULTIVATING CULTURE &
PRIORITIZING PURPOSE

www.aaasolutions.us

"Until we make the unconscious conscious, it will rule our lives and we will call it fate."

-Carl Jung

CHAPTER 5: DISRUPTING UNCONSCIOUS BIAS

The next building block will help participants define, manage, and disrupt unconscious bias and microaggressions in the workplace. This chapter will focus on unconscious bias and navigating these systematic thinking errors.

Unconscious/Implicit Bias Defined

So far, we have discussed prioritizing your purpose as it pertains to why DEI matters. We have discussed the importance of cultivating culture and laying the foundation for DEI in the workplace. We have even reviewed ways to develop emotional intelligence and create a more psychologically safe workplace. The next leg of the journey consists of becoming more aware of unconscious (also called implicit) bias and learning how to manage and disrupt bias as it arises. Before we define unconscious bias, let's see what unconscious bias looks like in action.

Caleb, the CEO of a local HVAC company, was discussing a vacancy in HR with his direct report, Jeff, the director of operations. They had narrowed the candidate pool to Steve and Melissa, who each had similar time with the company and comparable skills. When discussing Melissa's fitness for the position, Caleb said "I know she is looking to grow her family and may not be able to handle the workload of a promotion, so let's go with Steve." Caleb unknowingly allowed his unconscious bias to speak. Although Caleb's intent was not malicious, as he was talking to Jeff, the impact of his beliefs and decisions were certainly destructive.

Caleb was essentially saying that being pregnant or a mother threatens productivity and renders employee's incapable of performing at a high enough level to take on additional responsibility. These are very harmful beliefs to have as they will certainly lead to countless women being passed over for jobs, promotions, and stretch assignments where employees can work on projects outside the scope of their daily responsibilities.

This is an example of unconscious bias in the workplace: beliefs, thoughts, or actions that are expressed indirectly, where a person is unaware of their bias towards certain groups. It is important to note that unconscious bias operates subconsciously, meaning that one is unaware of what is happening. Unconscious bias is the set of learned or conditioned attitudes and stereotypes (widely held, oversimplified beliefs) that influence how we think and act.

Caleb's unconscious bias manifested when he implied that women are incapable of being mothers and simultaneously working at a high level. Unfortunately, not all bias is involuntary and subconscious. Let's review the opposite of unconscious bias.

Explicit Bias Defined

While unconscious bias involves someone being unaware of their biases, explicit bias involves someone being fully aware of and intentional in their negative actions and attitudes toward specific groups of people. Explicit bias is expressed directly and operates consciously in our minds. For example, let's talk about Joe, who is a Property Manager for a commercial real estate company. Part of Joe's role is to identify, screen, and select contractors to carry out various tasks. Imagine you are Joe's colleague and one day, you recommend Joe contact a certified Woman-owned business specializing in electrical work. Joe quickly responds by saying, "Women are not able to handle the physicality of being a contractor, so I don't think it will be a good fit for us."

This is an example of Joe making a deliberate decision to not work with certified Woman-owned businesses because he does not think they are capable of serving as a contractor for the property he manages. Joe has a deeply held and oversimplified image of women.

Although explicit bias is very damaging, this book will not focus on those who are committed to maintaining their separateness and ignorance but on people with a growth mindset willing to alter their thoughts and beliefs.

Two Systems of Thinking

Diverse, equitable, and inclusive cultures are aware of unconscious bias and actively work to mitigate bias. This work is about understanding what bias is and why it happens.

In his book *Thinking, Fast and Slow*, author, psychologist, and Nobel Prize laureate Daniel Kahneman, provides a great framework for understanding why bias occurs by examining the ways that humans process information through two systems of thinking.

In his overview of the two systems of thinking, Kahneman states,

- **"System 1 thinking** is fast, automatic, effortless, and occurs with no conscious sense of voluntary control. If someone asks you what 2 plus 2 is, your brain will likely supply the answer before you've given the question any conscious thought; that is System 1 at work."
- **"System 2 thinking,** in contrast, is slow, conscious, explicit, and deliberate. If someone asks you what 126 times 43 is, you would most likely need to engage in System 2 thinking to work out the answer."

According to Kahneman, we as humans prefer to engage System 1 thinking whenever possible. Here is what he had to say about our two systems of thinking and unconscious bias:

"When our brains are exposed to the same message or task repeatedly, that message or task will become automatic and virtually involuntary. This way of understanding our thought processes aligns with what neurologists know about the human brain and how learning occurs physiologically. In many cases, "outsourcing" our thinking to System 1 is beneficial for us. But what happens when our brains receive repeated messages that we might not want or consciously agree with? Well, that is when we get into unconscious bias, or implicit bias."

Since our brains prefer to use System 1 thinking, we often do not slow down long enough to question our assumptions and challenge our preconceived notions around a person, thing, or idea. If we were to engage System 2 thinking more often, we would be in a better position to diminish bias.

Common Biases

If you are a human, you have bias. That last sentence was so important that I would like to repeat it. If you are a human, you have bias. Yes, that includes you. You have biases if you are reading or listening to this right now. This does not make you a bad person, it simply makes you human. The goal is to become more aware of your biases, work to mitigate those biases, and certainly avoid sliding into the explicit bias category with your biases.

One of the first steps towards disrupting bias, is to be able to recognize and investigate the biases that you have. Awareness is key here. One personal bias that I possess and which I am fully aware of, is affinity bias. Affinity bias refers to preferring people with qualities similar to you or someone you think highly of. I know I have this bias because anytime I meet with someone who went to The Kelley School of Business at Indiana University Bloomington (go Hoosiers!), I instantly feel a strong connection with them. That connection often leads to building trust and therefore providing preferential treatment compared to other connections of mine who don't identify as proud Hoosiers.

Isn't it funny how we automatically assume someone is good because we share a school, fun fact, or hometown with them? This is how many of us are. This requires me to be intentional with investigating my assumptions with people I have an affinity towards. I am not saying to assume someone is not trustworthy simply because you want to avoid affinity bias, but I am saying that questioning our assumptions is mandatory for disrupting bias.

Let's look at some of the most common types of bias and, as we review each one, ask yourself if you've ever exhibited any of these behaviors. Remember, this is not about shame or guilt, but about growth and awareness. These can apply at home or at work as well.

- **"Affinity** – Preference for people who share qualities with you or someone you like"
- **"Anchoring** – Tendency to rely too heavily on the first piece of information offered when you are making decisions"
- **"Attribution** – Tendency to attribute other people's successes to luck or help from others and attribute their failures to lack of skill or personal shortcomings"
- **"Beauty** – Assumptions about people's skills or personality based on their physical appearance and tendency to favor people who are more attractive"
- **"Confirmation** – Selective focus on information that supports your initial opinion(s)"
- **"Conformity** – Tendency to be swayed too much by the views of other people"
- **"Contrast** – Assessment of two or more similar things by comparing them with one another rather than looking at their individual merits"
- **"Gender and Orientation** – tend to prefer one gender and/or orientation over another"
- **"Halo** – Focus on one particularly positive feature about a person that clouds your judgment"

- **"Horns** – Focus on one particularly negative feature about a person that clouds your judgment"

Do any of those biases resonate with you? Can you think of a time when you demonstrated one or maybe two or three of those common biases? I know I can, and I know I will have to continue to be intentional about not falling into those biased thoughts in the future.

Think about how these biases can impact people at work. Imagine being a recruiter or hiring manager, and you often suffer from beauty bias. Instead of bringing in the best candidates for the job, your perception of their overall skill set is skewed due to how attractive they are. Or maybe you are an aspiring C-suite executive hoping for a promotion. Only to get told by a close friend in Sr. Leadership, Sarah, that the CEO, Jasmine, seems to be displaying attribution bias towards you because Jasmine believes your success is due to your relationship with Sarah. Sarah also mentioned that Jasmine seemed to be overly fixated on the time you missed that deadline last year, and she tells you that from Jasmine's perspective, the mishap was attributed to your lack of project management skills.

Everything from performance evaluations to prescribing medication can be negatively impacted due to bias. Although each situation will be different, the consequences for bias at work can be significant. There are also biases that pertain specifically to underrepresented groups. Here are some of those marginalized groups that are affected most often when it comes to bias:

- Age (younger and older people)
- Gender (anyone who does not identify as a straight male)
- Race & Ethnicity (people of color)
- LGBTQIA+ Community
- Disability (persons with a disability)
- Veterans
- Religion (any religious beliefs outside of Christianity)

September 11, 2001 was a day that will live in infamy. Four US planes were hijacked, with two of the planes flying into the World Trade Center towers in New York City. One of the other planes hit the Pentagon in Arlington, Virginia, and the remaining hijacked plane failed to reach its intended target and crashed in Shanksville, Pennsylvania. Overall, almost 3,000 people were killed in these events.

Fear, immense sadness, confusion, and heartbreak quickly ensued nationally and worldwide. As a 9-year-old kid, this tragic day, would shape a bias of mine against people from the middle east well into adulthood. You see, the hijackers of the four commercial passenger airplanes were later connected with the Islamic extremist group, al Qaeda, which was founded by Osama bin Laden. Seeing images of the hijackers on news cycles nonstop would engrave a bias in my mind that people who looked like them (i.e. dark brown skin, hijab) were dangerous and that I should protect myself if I encountered someone at the grocery store or walking around my neighborhood who resembled the hijackers.

It was not until I began to study unconscious bias and look inward that I discovered my bias against people from the middle east, and it's source. You, too can illuminate your thinking and beliefs and begin exploring some of your biases and their origin. Let me show you how you can start to disrupt biases as they appear starting with awareness.

Disrupting Unconscious Bias

Hopefully, you understand that you should not feel bad for having bias. You are alive, so you have bias. If I sat in shame and guilt after discovering my bias against people from the middle east, that would not have helped me to begin disrupting the unconscious thoughts that would occasionally emerge. Instead, empathy wrapped in curiosity is a more effective approach.

For example, since I understood that bias is inevitable due to what we experience socially and through cognitive processes, I began to ask myself "why?" Why do I have these sentiments? Why did I make that assumption? This approach of intentionally trying to understand and release preconceived misconceptions helped me move toward discovering the root of those views. We must be willing to ask ourselves, what if I am wrong? What if this tall black man walking down the street is not a threat? Why did I clutch my purse at the store when the African American man was shopping near me, but I did not do the same when the younger white man in a hoodie was near me? These are the type of introspective questions one must begin to answer to disrupt bias.

In his book, *Everyday Bias,* Howard Ross shares ways to mitigate unconscious biases to create a different mental image. The 6-step framework created by Ross can be applied to many situations, especially talent management decisions. Here is an overview of each of the steps:

1. Assume that you have unconscious biases.
   - When you begin from a place of accepting that to be human is to have bias, it makes it easier to navigate bias.
2. Examine your worldview and conduct research on yourself.
   - This step is all about curiosity and self-awareness. Be willing to learn both about yourself and others.
3. Practice "Constructive Certainty."
   - This term refers to the importance of remembering that your thoughts and beliefs could be inaccurate. By acknowledging that having a skewed perception is possible, it opens the door for you to practice constructive certainty.
4. Explore Discomfort.
   - This work is not comfortable, so it is best to embrace the discomfort because that means you are growing.
5. Examine groups of people who might be missing from your life, that you have meaningful interactions with.

- This step challenges you to diversity your network so you can learn from people from all walks of life.

6. Seek feedback.

- Feedback is a gift that can lead to growth, but that can only happen if you intentionally seek it out.

Ross highlights the need to avoid defensiveness or denial. By having the courage and wisdom to investigate yourself, you enable yourself to grow. Ross challenges us to withhold judgments about what we see until we have more information on a situation or person. Different does not mean bad; it simply means different from you and your perspective or beliefs. Curiosity about people's reactions and behaviors in certain circumstances can be very insightful.

Ultimately, a growth mindset is required to navigate bias. We must be humble enough to admit that we do not have all the answers and we may be wrong. Otherwise, our biases will eventually become cemented in our minds as absolute truth and fact. This is one of many prerequisites for cultivating explicit bias. Working to improve your awareness around bias will be a very uncomfortable journey. Do not shy away from the discomfort, as that is where growth lives. There's a reason lifting weights at the gym doesn't usually feel good. You are growing your muscles. The same principle applies in the work of dismantling bias. As one of my favorite authors, Brene Brown, often states, "There is power in vulnerability" so let's all work to harness our power and use it for good through our willingness to be vulnerable and get comfortable with the uncomfortable.

In his book, Ross references research from the University of Virginia that discovered that when we diversify our exposure to people, especially those who are members of the groups we have biases about, "over time, the bias starts to dissipate." Since our biases are typically rooted in incomplete information and fear, spending meaningful time with people who are different than us can help paint a more complete picture of who others are. With the clarity of more information on others in mind, it is easier to release the fear that often comes with the unknown regarding other people.

Research has also shown that "racial bias is the greatest where racial diversity is the least". Start seeking out experiences that expose you to people and communities that deviate from what you have come to associate as "normal" in terms of physical ability, gender, race, ethnicity, religion, etc. Diversifying your network is a great way to disrupt our unconscious biases so we can better manage our biases instead of our biases managing us.

Unconscious Bias Training

In the aftermath of the George Floyd murder in May 2020, many businesses rushed to put out DEI statements and began seeking unconscious bias training shortly after. Now as a keynote speaker, consultant, and trainer, I highly recommend training so people can learn and grow. However, one-off unconscious bias training is not effective and does not produce lasting, sustainable change.

According to this article by Culture Amp, titled, "How effective is unconscious bias training?", "research has shown that if done poorly [unconscious bias training] can cause significant backlash and deepen issues of bias in the workplace. Moreover, there is a lack of consistent evidence that shows that UB training has positive, long-term impacts. While there are some cases where training can be effective, it is *never* an appropriate first or only solution to DEI challenges."

There is a reason why unconscious bias is just now being covered in this book. It is difficult to have unconscious bias training that has long-term effects without laying the foundation for DEI in general. Before discussing stereotypes and discrimination, people must know the difference between equity and equality. Additionally, we must be

equipped with an adequate vocabulary before effectively discussing what can be very polarizing topics regarding bias.

People do not know what they do not know. Training in general can fill that void, but it must be done right. A comprehensive DEI strategy coupled with training and development opportunities are the key, not one-off trainings with no plan for follow-up.

Here are some things you can do to increase the effectiveness of unconscious bias training.

- Measure what matters
  - Setting goals that are specific, measurable, attainable, relative, and time-sensitive (SMART) helps you focus on what exactly you want to accomplish and why.
  - According to the article by Culture Amp referenced above, "simply being aware of our biases doesn't change them. Ensure that any UB training program you consider focuses on equipping attendees with actionable strategies for managing bias. This may seem obvious, but one study found that only 10% of training programs shared strategies that attendees could use to mitigate bias."
- Work with an experienced DEI advisor and/or consultant
  - Leveraging someone who has expertise in this field can help you avoid many potholes and detours on your DEI journey. Shameless plug, but my firm (AAA Solutions) is more than happy to help you with your training and consulting needs
- Recognize the behaviors you want to be replicated.
  - Acknowledgment and recognition go a long way in keeping people motivated and productive. And since we often get more of what we recognize, it is important to celebrate and shout out the vulnerable people on your team, committed to self-awareness, and engaged in courageous conversations.

Unconscious Bias & DEI

As we begin to close this chapter, I want to ensure we are connecting the dots between DEI - fostering a culture of belonging - and the impact of disrupting unconscious bias. Embracing diversity of thought and ensuring people feel a strong sense of belonging at work creates a more inclusive work environment, and when people feel included at work, it enhances organizational effectiveness.

A 2020 McKinsey report on diversity in companies found that those in the top 25% for racial diversity among managers were 36% more likely to have financial returns above their industry mean; those in the top quartile for gender diversity in management were 25% more likely.

Research from Harvard Business Review also shows that collective intelligence is more than twice as important as individual team members' intelligence in determining team performance and that gender-diverse teams are smarter than those that are not gender-diverse. In addition, racially diverse teams avoid groupthink, make fewer errors in recalling relevant information, and work harder.

When people are held back or discriminated against in any way, that directly attacks engagement and belonging at work. That is exactly what unrecognized unconscious bias can lead to: the adverse treatment of people from marginalized groups. Discrimination can easily occur at work when we hold various stereotypes and act on those positions with bias. This process requires change, and we typically do not look forward to change as humans. However, being willing to change can be the ripple effect necessary to make waves down the road, not only at work, but in our personal lives as well. If you strive to lead with inclusivity, then you must be intentional with equity, which means people are treated fairly and respectfully. Fairness and respect can only take root when unconscious bias is held at bay.

"The concept of unconscious bias training itself was largely created to protect against legal liability for bias within organizations – not as a strategy to drive equitable experiences for all employees".

- Aubrey Blanche
Culture Amp's Senior Director of Equitable Design, Products & People

THE BUILDING BLOCKS OF BELONGING

5 STEPS TO CREATING A DIVERSE, EQUITABLE, AND INCLUSIVE CULTURE

BY ANDREW ADENIYI

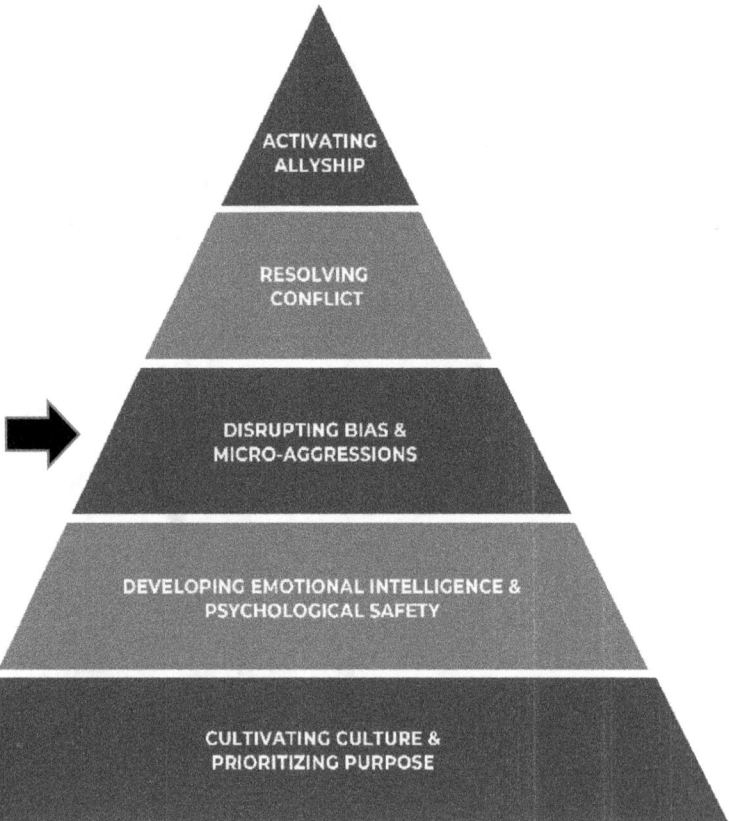

ACTIVATING ALLYSHIP

RESOLVING CONFLICT

DISRUPTING BIAS & MICRO-AGGRESSIONS

DEVELOPING EMOTIONAL INTELLIGENCE & PSYCHOLOGICAL SAFETY

CULTIVATING CULTURE & PRIORITIZING PURPOSE

www.aaasolutions.us

CHAPTER 6: MANAGING MICROAGGRESSIONS

This building block will help readers define and manage microaggressions in the workplace. This chapter will focus on awareness of microaggressions and how to engage in those crucial conversations.

Bias Review

When it comes to unconscious bias, we have discussed how biases are learned attitudes or stereotypes, and these subconscious thoughts can subtly yet severely impact members of marginalized groups. The stereotypes we hold on to involuntarily cause us to have oversimplified images of people and things.

Although it may be unintentional, our unconscious bias can manifest in our initial reactions, feelings, and judgments. When we let these assumptions run rampant in the workplace, it often can lead to what we call microaggressions. This chapter will define microaggression and discuss why it's considered a subtle act of exclusion. We will explore some examples of microaggressions in the workplace and review best practices around what to do and what not to do when experiencing those situations. Lastly, we will deep dive into tools for managing microaggressions in the workplace.

What are Microaggressions?

Tomi is a highly dynamic Black woman and lawyer. She has worked her way up the corporate ladder and recently became a Partner at one of the most prestigious law firms in the country. As one of two female Partners at the firm, she is very proud of her accomplishments but well aware of the challenges she will face due to her gender. Law is a predominantly white and male industry, and her firm is no exception.

During a trip to the office of a prospective client, she brought three team members (all subordinates) with her. All the people she brought were male, and two, Joseph and Evan, were white. Tomi had not interacted with this client before meeting with them but was eager to learn more about their business and how her team would approach the meeting.

As Tomi and her three colleagues entered the large conference room, the CEO of the company they were visiting, Matt, and COO, Austin, greeted them. From the beginning, Tomi noticed that Austin and Matt focused most of their attention on the two white males on her team, Joseph and Evan. In fact, Matt only extended his hand to introduce himself to Evan and Joseph and proceeded to direct his questions and comments toward them, assuming they were in charge.

What Tomi experienced during this brief but memorable exchange was a microaggression. Microaggressions are moments of subtle and/or unintentional discrimination against members of a marginalized group. Although Matt and Austin did not intend to offend anyone from the law firm, introducing themselves first to the males in a mixed-gender and mixed-race group and prioritizing communication with them because they assumed they were in charge harmed Tomi.

Microaggressions, as you can imagine, can be very nuanced and unique depending on context. However, regardless of the situation, the impact communicates similar themes. These small, hurtful interactions over time can have serious consequences. For example, the results of this microaggression on Tomi: she felt invisible and inadequate for leadership because of her race and gender. Repeated microaggressions like this can have a compounding effect and communicate to Tomi that she does not belong and is not enough.

When you think of a microaggression, think about a mosquito bite or paper cut. It is not the end of the world if you get bitten, but several persistent bites can start to do damage. The same is true for a paper cut. Although nagging and uncomfortable, chances are you will not be severely negatively impacted by a single paper cut. However, repeated paper cuts can cause increased pain over time.

Another thing to remember is that microaggressions can be a form of illegal discrimination in the workplace. So, in addition to morale and engagement issues with people who are constantly on the receiving end of microaggressions, you also have the legal risk side to consider. Ultimately, we should all be working to prevent and avoid workplace discrimination, including education on microaggressions and managing them as they arise.

Explicit vs. Implicit

As discussed in the previous chapter, bias can be implicit or explicit. The same is true for microaggressions. The example we shared about Tomi in the conference room was implicit. There was no intent to cause harm to Tomi or question her authority. Our example would have been explicit (rather than implicit) if Evan intentionally disregarded Tomi and refused to engage with her despite learning about her role as a Partner for her law firm. This chapter will focus on microaggressions being implicitly stated and will not focus on explicitly racist or discriminatory comments or actions.

Chester M. Pierce, a Harvard psychiatrist, coined the term microaggressions. What started in the early 1970s as a way to describe offenses towards African Americans eventually began to apply to women and any marginalized group. Regardless of intent, if your actions, comments, or behavior leads to someone being excluded based on characteristics of their identity, it could be considered discrimination.

Some may say that microaggressions feel like an assault on free speech. Others may feel like people are overly sensitive and need to be less fragile. Ultimately, company policies and codes of conduct typically outline what is and is not acceptable in the workplace. Discrimination of any sort is usually at the top of the list of things that will not be tolerated. That said, anything that goes against a culture of belonging in the workplace should have clear consequences as a violation of company policy. Awareness is power, and creating more culturally aware environments can improve employee engagement.

Subtle Acts of Exclusion (SAE)

Like unconscious bias, microaggressions can lead to multiple people looking at the same thing but seeing something differently. This difference in perception is where diversity in the workplace is helpful. It improves awareness and deepens understanding of how other people perceive things. Instead of opting for the fast and automatic system one thinking we mentioned in the last chapter, we need to slow down, pause, and engage in system two thinking to be more deliberate and thoughtful in our comments and behavior.

Let's look at how to let go of preconceived notions and create a different picture. In the book titled *Subtle Acts of Exclusion* by Tiffany Jana and Michael Baran, the authors argue for referring to microaggressions as subtle acts of exclusion (SAE). The authors unpack how microaggressions can communicate that the impact of the hurtful comments is not significant. So, to highlight the effects of exclusionary comments, SAE was introduced by the authors.

Here is an overview of each component of SAE:

- **Subtle:** These can be difficult to identify and uncomfortable to discuss.
- **Acts:** Based on what people say and do.
- **Exclude:** Lead to exclusion rather than belonging.

According to the book, here are the common SAE types in the workplace:

- You are invisible
- You (or people like you) are inadequate
- You are not an individual
- You do not belong
- You are not normal
- You are a curiosity
- You are a threat
- You are a burden

Our earlier example of Tomi's situation left her feeling invisible, inadequate, and like she did not belong. Let's explore another example of some of these common SAE types in the workplace.

"Where are you from?" Celeste asked Carlos, the middle-aged, brown-skinned male supplier.
"South Bend, Indiana," Carlos replied.
"No, where are you really from?" Celeste quickly replied.

This short exchange has already communicated to Carlos that he is a curiosity and not "normal." Due to the color of his skin, facial features, etc., Celeste could not fathom that he was truly from Indiana, even though Carlos was born and raised in the Midwest and had only visited family in Mexico once in his lifetime. Although Carlos considers himself mixed, which can be challenging to categorize, Celeste questioning Carlos' heritage and ethnicity is frustrating to him.

Carlos is used to these types of exchanges, but as with a paper cut, enough of them consistently over time can harm anyone. Carlos's father is Irish, and his mother is Hispanic, so he usually cuts people slack for questioning his identity, but on this particular occasion, the assumption that he cannot possibly be from the United States of America makes him feel like he is less of an American because of how he looks despite being born in the country.

What begins with curiosity can end with communicating to others, "You are not normal." I want to be clear that being curious is not the problem. Curiosity is key when it comes to leaning into courageous conversations and learning more about others that are different than you. However, you should strive to not let your curiosity feel like they are not normal and that they do not belong.

Hair Bias and Microaggressions

According to the article "How Hair Discrimination Affects Black Women at Work" by Janice Gassam Asare, Ph.D. in Harvard Business Review

- "Black women's hair was two-and-a-half times more likely to be perceived as unprofessional."
- "More than half of the Black women surveyed felt like they had to wear their hair straight in a job interview to be successful. Two-thirds reported that they had changed their hair for a job interview."
- "One-fifth of the Black women surveyed between the ages of 25 and 34 had been sent home from work because of their hair."

- "A quarter of the Black women surveyed believe they were denied a job because of their hair."

This article unpacks a very common form of SAE toward women of color in the workplace regarding hair bias. Hair bias can often negatively impact safety, perceived feelings of belonging, and career advancement opportunities. To adequately address hair bias that manifests in microaggressions like this, leaders should review policies, invest in training and education, and create a culture of soliciting feedback. Ultimately, all employees deserve to feel a sense of belonging at work. Taking some of these steps can help women of color, in particular, to not feel isolated, excluded, or limited in growth due to their hair.

PADE Explained

You may ask yourself, "What do I do if I witness or hear an SAE?" Or maybe you're curious about what you should say if you are on the receiving end of an SAE. Let's review a few frameworks that can help you regardless of your role in the SAE.

PADE is an acronym that stands for:

- **(P) Pause the action:** Take a deep breath and self-regulate emotions
- **(A) Assume positive intent:** Curiosity will lead to more open communication
- **(D) Describe your perspective:** Share your thoughts, emotions, and preferences
- **(E) Expect Progress:** Be gentle on the person, tough on the behavior

This framework applies to instances where you were on the receiving end of the SAE, or you observed it. Pausing the action allows you to compose yourself and collect your thoughts. A phrase as simple as "Hold on" or "Time-out" can do the trick. Assuming positive intent is about avoiding defensiveness and encouraging collaboration. A phrase like "I know you did not mean any harm by this, but..." would be appropriate.

Describing your perspective revolves around engaging in a courageous conversation to promote learning and building stronger relationships. Lastly, expecting progress is based on clarifying expectations and following up as needed to collect ongoing feedback. The key is to be gentle on the person, but tough on the behavior

Let's take a look at an example SAE and apply it to the PADE framework:

Black person's hair being professional

- **Pause the action:** "Excuse me, I would like to address the comments you just shared."
- **Assume positive intent:** "I know you did not mean any harm to her, but..."
- **Describe your perspective:** "Some Black women often feel like their hair is not deemed professional and that their hair is perceived as strange. I know that comments like the ones you shared could make some Black women feel excluded and insecure."
- **Expect progress:** "I would hate for you to make remarks like that again in the future and upset someone, so I just want to ensure that you are aware."

Stereotypes + Bias/Prejudice = Discrimination

Below is an example of bias and microaggressions that I saw years ago on social media:

White locksmith:

- "Is this your house?"
- "Are you moving (on) up?"
- "Are you new to this area?"
- "I hope this isn't culture shock for you."
- "Follow me to talk numbers."
- "What do you do for a living?"
- "How good are you at math?"

Black locksmith:

- "Congratulations on the new house!"
- "Do you have kids?"
- "How are they adjusting?"
- "Today's the first day of school, right?"
- "I'm happy for you."
- "Can you show me which locks you'd like to update?"

The author of this post, who I do not know, shared after the post that this was an example of how she experiences life as a Black woman. The locksmith's initial doubts about her being the owner of the home is insinuated by the opening question and then that question is followed up by an assumption of her "moving on up". The culture shock comments and the comments inquiring around her competence in math communicate to this lady that she is not normal, and she is not adequate. In this situation, all she wanted was for the locksmith to change the locks, give her the keys, and go on his way, i.e., completing the service she paid for. Instead, that service came with microaggressions driven by unconscious bias and rooted in racism.

Impact > Intent

One of the tricky parts about SAE is that intentions often come from a good place. People usually do not intend to offend a team member who does not celebrate Christmas by telling them, "I hope you have a Merry Christmas," at the end of their email exchange. When you misread someone's name and fail to attempt to get it right or even laugh at it, the impact can be damaging despite your good intentions. This example of an SAE can communicate "you are invisible" and "you are not normal." Ultimately, regarding SAE, the focus is not on the intent but the impact.

When you overly praise someone with a disability because you are impressed by something they have accomplished, your intent is acknowledgment and genuine surprise. However, the impact can be "I am not normal." It does not matter that you had good intentions. What matters is those good intentions ultimately resulted in a negative impact on someone else.

Thinking before you speak and asking yourself who may feel like they do not belong by the comment(s) you want to make both go a long way in not excluding others. Remember that everyone has their preferences, so although these concepts are a good rule of thumb, they may not apply to everyone you encounter. Embrace the discomfort that can arise from these situations, as they can lead to growth if you have the right mindset. Avoid becoming defensive and prioritize creating a culture of belonging for all you encounter.

Remember Your ABCs

At one point or another, you will most likely be the person guilty of committing a SAE. When that moment comes, the key to navigating those uncomfortable interactions is to remember you're ABCs. This is an acronym that describes the following:

- (A) Acknowledge that feedback is a gift
- (B) Be curious
- (C) Commit to progress

Even if you do not agree with someone's perception of something you did or said, their perception is their reality. Furthermore, they had the courage to mention it to you, providing a learning opportunity that would not have otherwise presented itself. So, an appropriate response includes simply saying thank you. By thanking them for feedback, it validates their feelings and helps you avoid being defensive. This openness and gratitude allow for dialogue to continue as perceptions of safety increase.

Being curious is all about challenging assumptions. What about their comments and feedback can you take with you that will help you down the road? That simple question can put you in a position to be curious and empathetic rather than judgmental and offended.

Lastly, committing to progress is about having a growth mindset and continuously improving. This is where accountability is key. Own what you can, commit to improving, and follow up with the person or persons impacted by the SAE as needed. When we fail to follow this framework, we can exacerbate something called internalized oppression.

Internalized Oppression

Definitionally, internalized oppression is when "marginalized groups **unknowingly** accept or "buy in" to some of the **stereotypical or negative messages** promoted about them and act accordingly." Simply put, SAEs can cause people to anticipate further SAEs even when that may not be the case. In the book *Subtle Acts of Exclusion,* the authors use an example of a Black woman not keeping her natural hair for an upcoming interview due to fear of not getting the job because of her hairstyle. Over time, SAEs can make people second guess their actions and get in their heads. So whenever possible, it is important to validate someone's feelings, own what you can, be curious, and commit to doing better.

We all play a role in minimizing SAEs in the workplace. Our collective responsibility is to work towards being an ally who observes something and speaks up. We want to avoid being inactive bystanders because that only perpetuates the problem and further communicates to others that they are invisible. Progress can happen when we confront the initiator of SAEs with grace and communicate with respect.

In conclusion, although SAEs are tiny, they can cause significant damage in the workplace. Diversity will come if we strive to lead with inclusivity while being intentional with equity. However, diverse talent will not stay at your organization and perform to the best of their abilities if they are met with countless SAEs throughout the workweek. Despite the discomfort of addressing SAE, this resistance is truly a resource that can lead to transformation for a team. Although people from underrepresented groups will benefit most from elevating this work, all team members will benefit because employee engagement and an overall sense of belonging will rise for the organization, leading to higher performance overall.

"If you think you are too small to make a difference, try sleeping with a mosquito"
-Dalai Lama

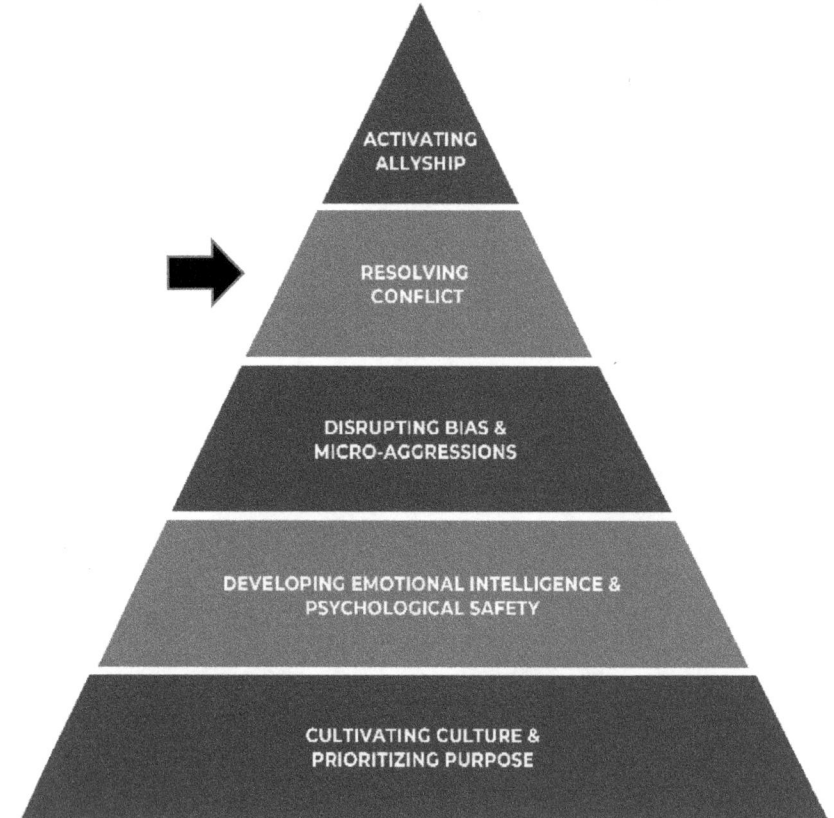

THE BUILDING BLOCKS
OF BELONGING

5 STEPS TO CREATING A DIVERSE, EQUITABLE,
AND INCLUSIVE CULTURE

BY ANDREW ADENIYI

ACTIVATING
ALLYSHIP

RESOLVING
CONFLICT

DISRUPTING BIAS &
MICRO-AGGRESSIONS

DEVELOPING EMOTIONAL INTELLIGENCE &
PSYCHOLOGICAL SAFETY

CULTIVATING CULTURE &
PRIORITIZING PURPOSE

www.aaasolutions.us

CHAPTER 7: RESOLVING CONFLICT

This building block will help participants better understand why conflict occurs and unpack ways to prevent, navigate, and resolve conflict in the workplace. Diversity is great, but when diverse perspectives come together, tension can occur. This is why organizations must be able to embrace conflict as long as it is healthy and productive.

Courageous Conversations

I like to think of courage as the desire and ability to pursue something that intimidates you. A conversation is simply a discussion between two or more people, exchanging information. Sounds simple enough, but having a courageous conversation at work can be one of the most uncomfortable things we do. Whether you're addressing a high performer who rubs their colleagues the wrong way or a poor performer who seems to have all the reasons to justify their substandard results, preparing for and effectively facilitating a courageous conversation is not something at which most people excel.

Part of the reason people dread having uncomfortable conversations is that many people lack the skill to resolve conflict. Oftentimes people are not adequately trained in conflict resolution and therefore do not handle those situations well or, even worse, they avoid having courageous conversations entirely. Some of us have also witnessed our parents or leaders at work poorly performing in conflict resolution, making it even more challenging to determine the best plan of attack to resolve conflict. Regardless of where you fall on the spectrum around comfort in having courageous conversations, this chapter will walk you through what conflict is, why resolving conflict matters, and some tools to prevent and resolve conflict in the workplace.

Conflict Defined

Conflict can sometimes be debilitating because the source of conflict is often a barrier to one's core needs, values, or goals. When something gets in the way of what you are striving for and working towards, it can result in intense emotions and strong feelings. Maslow's Hierarchy of Needs outlines the critical requirements for us to show up as our best selves. These needs include:

- Physiological needs
- Safety needs
- Love and belonging needs
- Esteem
- Self-actualization

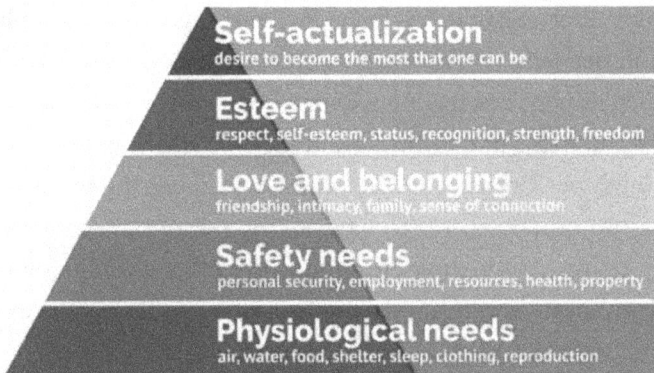

When someone or something threatens your ability to provide or protect yourself and others, this causes conflict. When your sense of connection and belonging with others is at risk, conflict can arise. And when you feel overlooked, held back, or overtly disrespected, it can negatively impact how you see yourself. However, if we are unaware of our needs, it will be difficult to properly handle conflict that stems from our unmet needs.

A key question to ask yourself and attempt to answer is, "Which core need is driving your conflict?" The answer to that will help you determine the right course of action. "Research published in Organizational Behavior and Human Decision Processes indicates that when one's identity is threatened, defensive psychological mechanisms are activated, leading to conflict, anger, and resentment." This is why conflict is considered an extended struggle or disagreement.

Being aware of your core values is also important to note. For example, if you determine that your core values are autonomy, innovation, and growth, anything threatening your freedom, creativity, and ability to learn will be unacceptable for you. This self-awareness alone will help you process and navigate conflict that may arise.

Choices & Conflict

According to the book titled *HBR Guide to Dealing with Conflict,* by Amy Gallo, there are 4 types of conflict:

1. Relationship (Personal disagreement)
2. Task (Disagreement over what the goal is)
3. Process (Disagreement over the means or process for achieving a goal)
4. Status (Disagreement over your standing in a group)

You may want to handle the situation in a particular way based on the type of conflict you are dealing with. For example, if you discover that the type of conflict you are having with a colleague is due to status on a project or deliverable, you may want to switch teams or clarify roles to begin to resolve the conflict. Status refers to a person's position and responsibility within a group. However, if the conflict is a relationship conflict with a vendor you see four times a year, you may determine that it is not worth your time to make the personal disagreement bigger than it needs to be.

Now that we know how to identify and categorize conflict, what are our choices for handling conflict? The good news about is that you have options. You can:

A) Do nothing,
B) Indirectly address the conflict,
C) Directly address the conflict, or
D) Exit the relationship.

For the sake of this chapter and book and to encourage courageous conversations, I will speak primarily about choosing option C) Directly addressing the conflict.

In the book *Conflict Resolution Playbook*, author Jeremy Pollack discusses the difference between conflict resolution and conflict management. Conflict management involves implementing processes and systems to minimize the negative effects of conflict, whereas conflict resolution reestablishes trust to rebuild the relationship. Managing conflict keeps it at bay and often serves as a legitimate option, especially in the short term, but resolving conflict focuses on solving problems to alleviate long-term tension. When possible, I recommend aiming to resolve conflict rather than manage, but managing conflict may be the better option depending on the situation.

One interesting component of conflict is that when we encounter it, our body often responds similarly to if we were in physical danger. That means we enter into fight or flight mode. Our brain detects danger, and therefore our mind and body begin to prepare to fight! No wonder why some of us often run from conflict. We are simply doing what our body and brain are telling us to do: protect ourselves. The key is to slow down, regulate your feelings, and have a courageous conversation once emotions are in check and you can engage in healthy dialogue.

Benefits of Conflict

In my conflict resolution trainings, I often ask participants to write all the reasons why conflict occurs on a post-it note. Typically people will share things like:

- Miscommunication
- Distrust
- Disrespect
- Lack of awareness
- Lack of clarity
- Stress

Ultimately, people can have completely different understandings of the same event which can be a common source of conflict. Luckily there are some benefits to conflict in the workplace. Below are some of those benefits:

- Healthy debates lead to more informed decisions
- Awareness of underlying issues that can lead to greater mutual understanding
- Can lead to innovation
- Can create a stronger sense of identity and confidence

Most organizations want to make the best decisions possible that will keep the organization innovative, relevant, and successful. These are things that conflict can positively influence if the conflict is healthy. Healthy conflict means that instead of being critical of an individual's character, ability, and value, the dialogue is focused on ideas, strategies, tactics, and goals. People with strong relationships rooted in trust are less likely to take personal offense to someone challenging their position or opinion. It is easier for team members to understand that the teammate has their best interest in mind but ultimately prioritizes making the best decision for the overall team and/or company. Without trust, contentious moments will likely fall into the category of unproductive and unhealthy conflict.

So, whether you are trying to build and maintain relationships, decrease your stress levels, or simply improve the frequency of collaboration inside your workplace, healthy conflict can be the catalyst you need to get there. In my first book, *The Circle of Leadership*, I define culture as "the unwritten, yet commonly shared set of beliefs that guide behavior." This definition is critical because culture influences behavior; if you can influence someone's behavior, you can influence their results.

Conflict Scenario

Leonard is the Director of HR for a nonprofit organization with about 50 employees. His day suddenly turns for the worst when he receives an email from a sales rep within the organization named Mandy. Mandy explained in her email that her boss, Fred, the VP of Sales for the company, was demeaning, disrespectful, and dismissive to her, and she was considering leaving the organization if his behavior did not change.

Alarmed by the urgent and upsetting nature of the email, Leonard immediately responded to Mandy asking to set up a time to chat about the situation further. During their coffee chat the next morning, Mandy explained to Leonard how Derrin tended to delegate things only to micromanage the work or, in some cases, take back responsibility he had delegated if he felt the task was being done differently than he would like. Mandy also mentioned how Derrin often interrupts her and other sales reps, regardless of whether they are meeting with coworkers or clients.

When Leonard asked if Mandy had approached Derrin about their working relationship, she said no because he overheard Derrin gossiping about a former employee who had a problem with his leadership style, and he ultimately began micromanaging the employee until they decided to quit. Mandy feared losing her job or that Derrin would retaliate if she brought this up to him. However, Mandy contemplated resigning anyway due to the stress but figured she would take her complaints to HR first in case the situation could be rectified.

Leonard ultimately took detailed notes from the conversation with Mandy and met with Derrin separately as well to hear his perspective. Leonard was surprised to hear from Derrin that he was shocked at the experiences Mandy had described and thought they had a great working relationship. Leonard followed up by facilitating a joint conversation with Derrin and Mandy where both sides could candidly and respectfully express how they were feeling and why.

At the conclusion of the conversation, both parties felt heard, seen, and valued. Derrin agreed to be more intentional with clarifying expectations upfront and providing the necessary resources to complete delegated work. Derrin was willing to change the frequency of check-ins and truly trust Mandy and others on the team to do great work once he could verify they were trained adequately. Mandy agreed to provide timely feedback to Derrin so he could be more aware of moments when he talked over her or was too in the weeds with work delegated to her.

Leonard also took this opportunity to bring in a speaker to train the entire company on courageous conversations and conflict resolution. By providing training to the team and clearly articulating the why behind the training, survey results indicated a greater sense of psychological safety and improvement in overall employee experience. Leonard was able to be an empathetic listener, curious consultant, and strategic executive in this scenario resulting in changed behavior and improved results.

Reflection questions

Rejecting ideas quickly will make people feel like Mandy: defensive, defeated, and demotivated to engage. When we stay open to others' ideas and truly consider their contributions and perspectives, people feel seen, heard, and valued even when you disagree. Sometimes the right answer for addressing conflict starts with asking the right questions. As scenarios arise in your workplace that need handling, here are some questions to ask yourself and anyone else involved in the conflict.

- What is the root cause of the conflict?
- Why did this conflict occur?
- What type of conflict is this?
- Should they look to manage this conflict or resolve it?
- What role did Emotional Intelligence (EQ) play in this conflict?
- How can developing EQ improve this situation?

Managing & Resolving Conflict

Now that we have reviewed what conflict is, why it occurs, and our options for resolving it, let's discuss some tools you can add to your toolkit to have courageous conversations. What is the key to effectively resolving conflict? The answer is P.P.E. Not the personal protective equipment you may be thinking about, but something just as critical for avoiding hazardous situations with workplace culture. P.P.E. is an acronym that stands for Preparation, Perform, and Evaluate.

Preparation: The scouting report (S.C.O.U.T.)

S: Set a goal

C: Conflict identification

O: Organizational context

U: Understand your counterpart

T: Timing is key

This phase of navigating conflict is about assessing the situation, setting aside time to have a conversation, and brainstorming how to approach the conversation. In football and other sports, a scouting report breaks down important information on your opponent and your intended plan of attack.

Although we do not want to view people we are talking to in the workplace as opponents, the premise of a scouting report still applies. You must set the stage for a productive and honest conversation which means you need to anticipate how they may respond to various questions and think through counter responses. Have your documentation ready to go so you can mention specifics as needed. You'll be much more confident heading into a tough conversation knowing you've done your homework.

Perform: Gametime (A.T.I.)

- Active Listening
- Third Chair Approach
- I Statements

Although preparation is key, you have to have the conversation at some point. You can prepare all you want, but the goal is to sit down and discuss the situation at hand promptly and appropriately. It is important to establish ground rules and expectations for the conversation upfront. You want to be calm, assertive, and compassionate during your courageous conversation.

Open-ended questions should be asked, and positive intent should always be assumed. Repeating back what you hear and being cognizant of your body language can demonstrate that you are actively listening. The Third Chair Approach about being tough on the behavior and gentle on the person. It frames the problem as something separate from the person so people can be less defensive. When you do this well, it creates a more collaborative environment.

"I" statements also help to decrease defensiveness. When you leverage I statements, you state what you feel, why you feel that way, and what you would prefer. For example, in our scenario earlier in the chapter with Derrin, many of Derrin's co-workers could have told him, "I feel underappreciated when you delegate things to me and take the responsibility back without giving me an opportunity to do the work myself. It makes me feel like you do not think I am smart enough or talented enough to do the job. I would prefer you spend more time upfront clarifying expectations, providing your thoughts, and then giving me more freedom to complete the work how I think is best. What are your thoughts on that?"

The goal here is to balance accountability and empathy. Inappropriate behavior can be addressed with candor while you are also actively listening and being supportive of expectations moving forward. Framing feedback using I statements makes the environment more conducive for problem solving.

Evaluate: Film Room

Your work is not complete after the conversation has been had. Like in sports, you must review the film and evaluate your performance. Being a detailed note-taker helps tremendously with follow-up. You want to ensure that whatever commitments were agreed on during the conversation are discussed later to verify that change has occurred and there is alignment with feedback and progress.

Reflect on the tone used during the conversation, your body language, and the body language of the person you were talking to. According to Albert Mehrabian's Rule, communication is 93% body language and tone, so be mindful of all the ways communication was transferred during the conversation.

Regardless of whether you are giving or receiving feedback, start positively by assuming positive intent, share your perspective using I statements, and be an active listener as you ask open-ended questions.

Remember to end your conversation with a summary and details regarding the next steps. Be willing to collaborate and make sure you prepare to perform. Expect conflict as your organization diversifies, but intentionally create a safe space to embrace healthy conflict. This will result in a more inclusive environment for all.

"Our ability to reach unity in diversity will be the beauty and the test of our civilization."

-Mahatma Gandhi

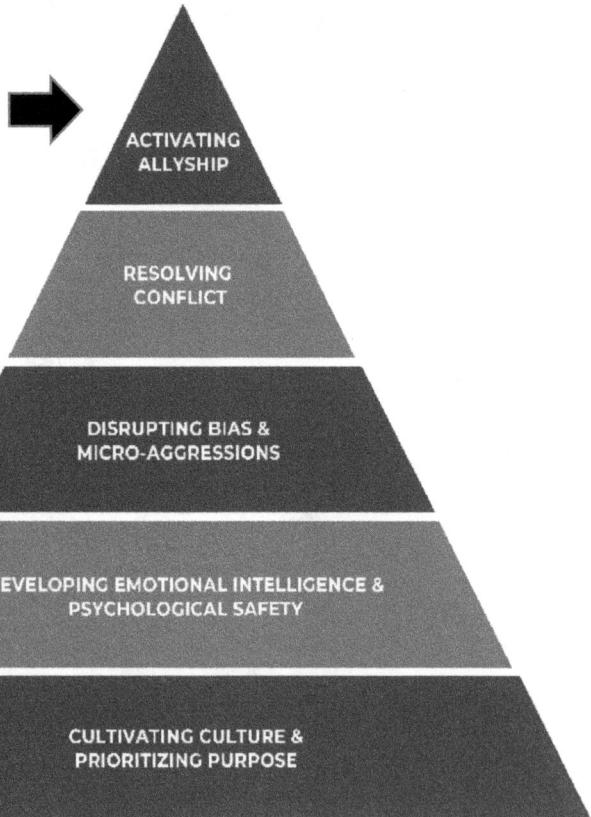

THE BUILDING BLOCKS OF BELONGING

5 STEPS TO CREATING A DIVERSE, EQUITABLE, AND INCLUSIVE CULTURE

BY ANDREW ADENIYI

ACTIVATING ALLYSHIP

RESOLVING CONFLICT

DISRUPTING BIAS & MICRO-AGGRESSIONS

DEVELOPING EMOTIONAL INTELLIGENCE & PSYCHOLOGICAL SAFETY

CULTIVATING CULTURE & PRIORITIZING PURPOSE

www.aaasolutions.us

CHAPTER 8: ACTIVATING ALLYSHIP

This building block will help participants better understand allyship, why it matters, and how to become an active ally in the workplace.

Allyship Explained

Everyone in your organization deserves to feel a sense of belonging at work. For that to happen, team members must feel like their diverse perspectives are valued, and their contributions are appreciated. *The Building Blocks of Belonging* has introduced topics that leaders can unpack to foster cultures where employees are engaged and encouraged to challenge the status quo.

Allyship is the conglomeration of all the previous building blocks put into action. Actively utilizing this pyramid will be a clear first step toward becoming an effective ally. In this book we discussed cultivating culture by prioritizing purpose. This building block challenged you to answer the question "why?" We also discussed the importance of developing emotional intelligence, creating psychological safety, and resolving conflict in the workplace. When we become more self-aware, we can better manage relationships by building trust and collaborating in meaningful ways.

We also covered the power of vulnerability when we are aware of our biases and actively work to disrupt those biases. Managing micro-aggressions was also covered in an attempt to educate and empower readers to create more inclusive environments. Ultimately, fostering a culture of belonging takes intentionality, courageous conversations, and empathy.

The last building block is all about sustaining momentum around creating a sense of belonging within your organization. This content will help develop inclusive leaders who ensure the workplace is equitable. This portion of the pyramid also prepares allies to take action and hold themselves accountable. This phase empowers you to create SMART goals around DEI. Let's briefly revisit the tragic murder of George Floyd in 2020 to set the stage for what being an active ally truly means.

Shortly after the murder of George Floyd, I remember my wife painting a vivid picture of the climate of society at the time, especially in America. Due to the murder being captured on video and the pandemic, my wife mentioned that the world had finally paused long enough to realize that there was litter all over the beach we call life. And although we may not have put the trash on the beach, we were collectively being faced with a pivotal choice. We could either continue to ignore the mess or begin doing our part in cleaning up the environment around us.

The mess I am speaking about in this instance is racism, social injustice, and police brutality. Luckily, as a country, we collectively leaned towards cleaning up the mess. Corporations, politicians, community leaders, activists, and more responded by attempting to become an active ally. When I say ally, I am describing someone who observes something and decides to speak and do something about it. Allies think before they speak and understand the difference between intent vs. impact. Allies are determined to be active participants (as opposed to inactive bystanders) by prioritizing making change for the betterment of others. Allies are selfless and motivated by guiding principles and values. Allies make the world a better place.

The police officers at the scene of the crime when George Floyd was murdered, failed to be active allies. Instead, they made a conscious decision to ignore their moral and ethical obligation to intervene. Instead of serving and protecting, they looked the other way and avoided holding their fellow officer accountable. Their choice to be passive bystanders to overt brutality made them complicit in George Floyd's murder. Their behavior is a perfect example of the opposite of an active ally.

We all have the ability to approach people with grace and respect when we see something that is wrong. It takes courage, initiative, and grit. The officers at the scene of that crime lacked all of the above and an innocent man lost his life as a result. Although this may be one of many extreme examples of what can happen when we choose to be passive bystanders rather than active allies, it demonstrates how catastrophic it can be when we do not hold ourselves and others accountable for their actions.

In the workplace, almost anything that makes someone feel like they do not belong is worthy of an ally stepping in. Remember to leverage the guidelines for speaking up that were covered in the chapter on micro-aggressions also known as subtle acts of exclusion. The P.A.D.E. framework reminds us to:

(P) Pause the action

(A) Assume positive intent

(D) Describe your perspective

(E) Expect Progress

Courage does not mean the absence of fear. You will likely be fearful when contemplating speaking up as an active ally. The key is to remember your why. Remember the purpose of stepping up and stepping in for those who need it most. How would you want someone to show up for you in moments when you feel excluded, overlooked, and disrespected?

Deep breathing, preparing your talking points, and being calm, confident, and assertive will help you serve as an active ally at work. Remember to be tough on the behavior but gentle on the person. You want to educate and enlighten them while supporting the person receiving the exclusionary comments or actions. As author Brene Brown says, "clear is kind" so be sure to be candid in your communication and compassionate in your delivery.

Like anything in life, practice leads to progress. The goal here is not perfection. The goal is to become more aware of situations where allyship is needed and to feel empowered to initiate these courageous conversations. Intentional acts of inclusion will help others feel like they belong, are safe, and are enough. Let's take a look at some numbers that indicate some groups of people who may need active allyship in the workplace.

Numbers Do Not Lie

My consulting firm, AAA Solutions, collected over 1000 survey responses between 2022 and 2023 from working professionals in various industries in the United States. The surveys captured self-disclosed demographic data along with ratings on a variety of workplace culture and DEI-related topics. When we filtered and compared scores for people who identified as African-American/Black vs. Not African-American/Black, we noticed some significant differences.

Survey respondents who identified as African-American/Black reported 13% less than those who identified as Not African-American/Black regarding overall sense of belonging in the workplace. That means on a 1-5 Likert scale, 1 being strongly disagree and 5 being strongly agree, African-American/Blacks had an average score of 3.86 compared to a score of 4.42 for non-African-American/Blacks. For context, almost 15% of respondents identified as African-American/Black and 85% identified as Not African-American/Black.

Here are some other interesting findings:

Represenation Matters

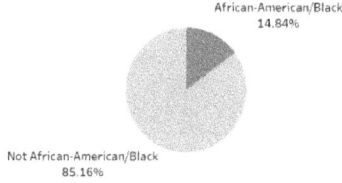

African-American/Black
14.84%

Not African-American/Black
85.16%

Overall Average Scores

	Belonging	Comfort	Advancement	Fair Compensation
African-American/Black	3.86 13%↓	3.87 9%↓	3.88 4%↓	3.28 18%↓
Not African-American/Black	4.42	4.25	4.05	4.00

Overall Average Scores Chart

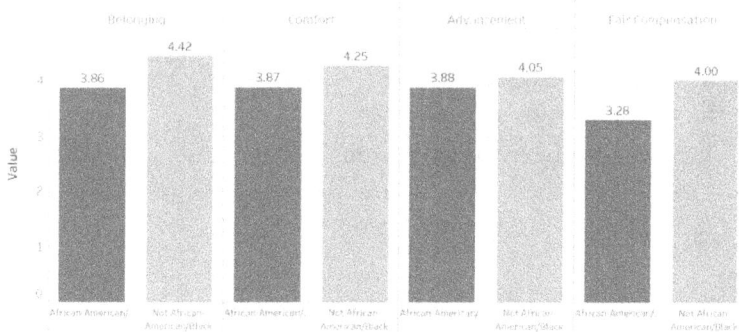

Regardless of whether we were evaluating belonging, comfort being themselves, opportunities for advancement, or fair compensation, African-Americans/Blacks evaluated their experience lower than non-African-Americans/Blacks. So when we talk about being an active ally, this is one data-driven way to become more aware of the importance and impact of allyship.

If you know that African Americans or other marginalized groups in your workplace are more likely to feel excluded, be extra mindful of intentionally including those individuals when possible. That could be as simple as seeking their feedback on various ideas and projects to learning more about team members who are different from you.

The Power of Privilege

Part of allyship is acknowledging your privilege and leveraging it in support of underrepresented or marginalized groups. To start wrapping your mind around the concept of power and privilege, here are two questions to consider:

What does it mean to have power?

- The ability or official authority to decide what is best for others.
- The ability to decide who will have access to resources.
- The capacity to exercise control over others.

What does it mean to have privilege?

- Privilege gives advantages, favors, and benefits to members of dominant groups (privileged) at the expense of members of target groups (marginalized).
- Privilege is unearned and is granted to people in the dominant groups whether they want those privileges or not, and regardless of their stated intent

Although I identify as a Nigerian-American and person of color which are marginalized identities, I myself still have an immense amount of privilege. The fact I am a male, able-bodied, straight, Christian, and come from a two-parent household, I get to receive unearned benefits that atheist women with a disability who identify as lesbian receives in society. The advantages that come with some of my identities should not make me feel guilty or ashamed, however, It is imperative to be aware of those benefits so I can leverage my privilege to be an ally to others.

Privilege can operate on various levels such as personal, interpersonal, cultural and institutional. Regardless of the level of privilege at hand, the goal is to remember that the privileges you have in this context are not due to things you have earned and therefore cannot be applied to others simply by members of marginalized groups working harder. Regardless of how hard a gay woman with a disability works, she will not be able to achieve the unearned benefits that straight, Christian males receive in society.

Here is a visual to help you better understand the difference between privileged and marginalized groups:

Privileged Groups vs. Marginalized Groups

Privileged Groups	Marginalized Groups
White People	Person of Color
Able-bodied	People with a physical, mental, emotional and/or learning disability; People living with AIDS/HIV+
Heterosexuals	Gay; Lesbian; Bisexual; Queer; Questioning
Males	Female; Intersex
Christians	Muslim, Jewish, Agnostic, Hindu, Atheist, Buddhist, Spiritual, LDS, Jehovah Witness, Pagan, …
Middle-aged	Younger; Older
English speaking	Use of "non-standard" English dialects; have an "accent"

When allies can acknowledge their privilege, it can propel you one step closer to becoming an active ally. When people have overlapping marginalized identities, we call this intersectionality which often brings on increased experiences of discrimination and oppression for marginalized people. A black woman for example cannot have those two identities (black and woman) exist independently of each other. This intersection can create a complex merging of oppression. My call to action for you is simple, become aware of your privileges and biases and commit to being an active ally to those who often get the short end of the stick pertaining to stereotypes, prejudice, discrimination, and oppression.

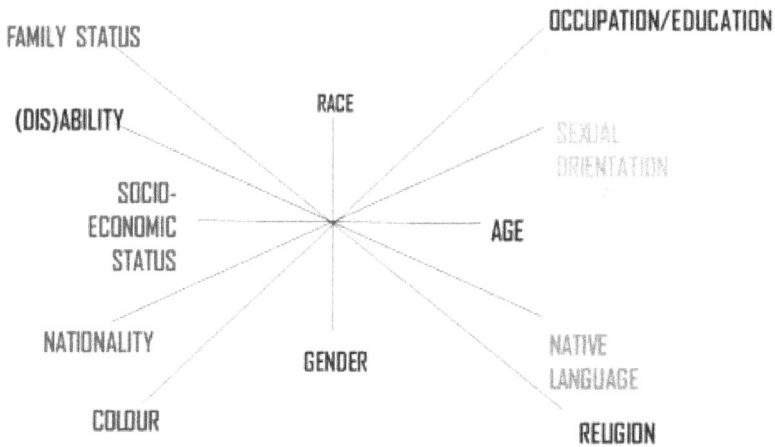

Acts of Allyship

Allyship does not need to be overly complicated. At its core, allyship is support for the rights of underrepresented groups of which you are not directly affiliated. For example, I can strive to be an active ally for people who have a disability. By being mindful of their needs and challenges, I can put myself in a better position to advocate for members of that group. Ensuring that they have representation at the decision-making table and are included in important projects can go a long way. It is important to mention that the support and advocacy for important projects should be for qualified individuals who were overlooked because of bias or exclusion. Allyship is not about handouts and providing opportunities to others simply due to their demographics.

According to this article titled "A Tale of Three Allies: What Does Allyship Look Like in Real Life?" by the NeuroLeadership Institute, here are three things you can do to practice allyship:

1. **Speak Up**
   - Just do it. Say something. Anything. Preferably something that shows support of those being discriminated against, but simply moving from bystander to ally is a critical step for enacting change and making a difference.

2. **Provide Opportunities**
   - Provide mentorship and stretch assignments to those who are different than you. Sharing opportunities for growth with marginalized groups can go a long way in advocating for those who oftentimes need it most.

3. **Challenge the status quo**
   - Being an ally means helping others feel psychologically safe in the workplace. Encouraging others to speak up, calling out exclusionary or biased practices and policies, and uplifting uncommon or innovative perspectives can all be powerful acts of allyship.

Acts of allyship do not need to be overly complicated. They just need to be acts. Something that you say or do. Amplify the ideas of others, advocate for what you know is right, and hold others accountable when needed. For additional ideas on how to be an active ally, check out https://guidetoallyship.com/.

Below are some of the ways the site describes how to be an ally:

- Practice perspective-taking
- Leverage your privilege
- Amplify the voices of the oppressed
- Stand up, even when you feel scared, and de-center yourself.
- Understand that your education is up to you

It's important to note that you should avoid self-proclaiming that you are an ally. Being an active ally is something you strive for but ultimately something that you get crowned by others. Focus on doing

the work for the right reasons and for the right people. Let's look at some data from Harvard Business Review that explores the intersection of allyship, black women, and psychological safety:

- "More than 80% of white women and men say they see themselves as allies to people of color at work. But less than half of Black women feel that they personally have strong allies at work." (According to Lean In's report, The State of Black Women in Corporate America, 2020)

- Black women are substantially more likely than white women — and just as likely as white men — to say that they are interested in becoming top executives. (According to Lean In's report, The State of Black Women in Corporate America, 2020)

- Black women receive nearly nine times as much feedback that's not actionable compared to white men under 40.

In conclusion, an ally is an observer who speaks up. The call to action to be an ally is clear, and you have two choices once you become aware of a situation that calls for an active ally.

1. Be a Bystander
2. Be an Ally

The choice is yours, and I encourage you all to choose wisely. You never know when you'll be the one in need of someone to choose the more courageous path. Focus on awareness, move towards action, and commit to being an advocate that holds others accountable.

Everyone's sense of belonging will improve when we all lean in and commit to cultivating a better work environment.

Thank you for reading. I hope you have enjoyed the contents of this book.

With Gratitude,

Andrew Adeniyi
Author | Consultant | Speaker

"If you are neutral on situations of injustice, you have chosen the side of the oppressor"

-Desmond Tutu

ABOUT THE AUTHOR

Andrew Adeniyi is a a first-generation Nigerian American and the CEO & Founder of AAA Solutions; a consulting firm that provides business strategy, workplace culture, and Diversity, Equity & Inclusion (DEI) consulting and training services. Andrew obtained his bachelor's degree in Entrepreneurship and Corporate Innovation from the Kelley School of Business at Indiana University Bloomington. He went on to complete his Master of Science from Michigan State University in Management, Strategy & Leadership. Lastly, Andrew received a certificate in DEI in the Workplace from The Muma College of Business at The University of South Florida.

With over 10 years of executive level management experience, Andrew has helped dozens of clients improve their employee engagement and create a sense of belonging within their organizations. Andrew currently resides just outside of Indianapolis, Indiana with his wife and three children. He published his first book titled *The Circle of Leadership* in the Summer of 2020 and it serves as an entrepreneurial framework on how to create and leverage culture.

Andrew Adeniyi

REFERENCES

INTRODUCTION

PAGE   REFERENCE

v   Deloitte, "Inclusive Mobility: How Mobilizing a Diverse Workforce Can Drive Business Performance", https://www2.deloitte.com/content/dam/Deloitte/us/Documents/Tax/us-tax-inclusive-mobility-mobilize-diverse-workforce-drive-business-performance.pdf

CHAPTER 1

PAGE   REFERENCE

3   Stanford Graduate School of Business, Note on Organizational Culture, https://hbsp.harvard.edu/product/OB69-PDF-ENG

6   Culture Amp, 2023, "Managing Burnout: 3 Ways to Support Employee Wellbeing", https://www.cultureamp.com/blog/managing-burnout?utm_campaign=AP%3APeople%20Geekly%20Newsletter%7CTe%3Ademand_gen%7CT%3Aplatform%7CP%3Afullplatform%7CR%3Aglobal&utm_medium=email&_hsmi=224194247&_hsenc=p2ANqtz-9W4u84h2MTvCMBQ7wsinjlcM21twY_c_ch_RiqmgXg-20DYh_ov8FJIxXZHfiyL3V1yIrHFEcF0rA9f4u8kMArfxImgQ&utm_content=224166068&utm_source=hs_email

9   Harvard Business Review, "The Other Diversity Dividend", https://hbr.org/2018/07/the-other-diversity-dividend

10   Center for Creative Leadership, "How an Ownership Mentality Supports Cultural Transformation", https://www.ccl.org/articles/leading-effectively-articles/ownership-mentality-cultural-transformation/?utm_source=external-email&utm_medium=email&utm_campaign=global_marketing_leading-effectively_august312022%20(1)&utm_content=&partnerref=email&spMailingID=72016545&spUserID=NTM2MzYzMDIxMDE0S0&spJobID=2252569515&spReportId=MjI1MjU2OTUxNQS2

CHAPTER 2

PAGE   REFERENCE

17   Society for Human Resource Management, "Employment Rate Rising For
        People with Disabilities", https://www.shrm.org/topics-
        tools/news/inclusion-equity-diversity/employment-rate-rising-people-
        disabilities#:~:text=The%20unemployment%20rate%20for%20people,for
        %20people%20without%20a%20disability.

19   FlashPoint Leadership, "What Can Leaders do to Counteract the Great
        Depression?", https://www.flashpointleadership.com/blog/what-can-
        leaders-do-to-counteract-the-great-
        resignation?utm_campaign=2021%20Blog&utm_medium=email&_hsmi=
        178797096&_hsenc=p2ANqtz-
        _TPeuD22tbcQ_HtO_y6fcwyKQY8Zhos7t7vpm9C_YsyiKe-
        jcuZuY3fM4b94eMsgRvqtZq_lx0l8sqL9Fpw0cALDoN2Q&utm_content
        =178797096&utm_source=hs_email

CHAPTER 3

PAGE   REFERENCE

31   Positive Psychology, "Emotional Intelligence Frameworks, Charts,
        Diagrams, & Graphs" by Leslie Riopel,
        https://positivepsychology.com/emotional-intelligence-frameworks/

33   Center for Creative Leadership, "The Importance of Empathy in the
        Workplace", https://www.ccl.org/articles/leading-effectively-
        articles/empathy-in-the-workplace-a-tool-for-effective-leadership/

34   YouTube Video, "Leading with Emotional Intelligence in the Workplace",
        Carolyn Stern, https://youtu.be/OoLVo3snNA0?si=9iGi_epm3305kJtm

34   YouTube Video, "Daniel Goleman Introduces Emotional Intelligence",
        Big Think, https://youtu.be/Y7m9eNoB3NU?si=DW-W3hz64LW9Y21T

34   Positive Psychology, "Emotional Intelligence Skills and How to Develop
        Them", https://positivepsychology.com/emotional-intelligence-skills/

35   Positive Psychology, "Emotional Intelligence Skills and How to Develop
        Them", https://positivepsychology.com/emotional-intelligence-skills/

37   Harvard Business Review, "The Young and the Clueless" by Bunker, Kram, and Ting, https://hbr.org/2002/12/the-young-and-the-clueless

38   Center for Creative Leadership, "The Importance of Empathy in the Workplace", https://www.ccl.org/articles/leading-effectively-articles/empathy-in-the-workplace-a-tool-for-effective-leadership/

CHAPTER 4

PAGE   REFERENCE

49   Culture Amp, "Company Culture 101", https://www.cultureamp.com/blog/company-culture-101?utm_campaign=AP%3APeople%20Geekly%20Newsletter%7CD%3A2022_05_09%7CTe%3Ademand_gen%7CT%3Aplatform%7CP%3Afullplatform%7CR%3Aglobal&utm_medium=email&_hsmi=212386468&_hsenc=p2ANqtz-_k267KxfT2kTQPKDmZwNZhWiik5wCuxWKH0OAYn24Z170b5hmvbH84V-TUPvOo_LQFVuaNHf9rzhjkFVZvkIne5ICpMA&utm_content=21220059&utm_source=hs_email

49   Columbia University Libraries, "Job Satisfaction and Employee Turnover Intention: What does Organizational Culture Have to Do It?", https://academiccommons.columbia.edu/doi/10.7916/D8DV1S08

53   Duhigg, Charles, "How Google Built a Better Team", https://www.youtube.com/watch?v=v2PaZ8Nl2T4

53   Catalyst, Workplaces that Work for Women, https://www.catalyst.org/research/workplace-inclusion-covid-19/

CHAPTER 5

PAGE   REFERENCE

66   Thinking, Fast and Slow, Daniel Kahneman, April, 2023.

73   Culture Amp, "How Effective is Unconscious Bias Training?",
        https://www.cultureamp.com/blog/unconscious-bias-
        training?utm_campaign=AP%3APeople%20Geekly%20Newsletter%7CD
        %3A2022_04_25%7CTe%3Ademand_gen%7CT%3Aplatform%7CP%3A
        fullplatform%7CR%3Aglobal&utm_medium=email&_hsmi=210947880&
        _hsenc=p2ANqtz-_8Qv4ziVDLsWrWMc-
        TNf0yFRuW5kQ2GIP0Hdnc5RHIq-

73   Harvard Business Review, "Diversity Policies Rarely Make Companies
        Fairer, and They Feel Threatening to White Men",
        https://hbr.org/2016/01/diversity-policies-dont-help-women-or-
        minorities-and-they-make-white-men-feel-threatened

74   Harvard Business Review, "Unconscious Bias Training That Works",
        https://archive.ph/i9ces#selection-1325.0-1325.772

74   McKinsey & Co., "Diversity wins: How inclusion matters.",
        https://www.mckinsey.com/featured-insights/diversity-and-
        inclusion/diversity-wins-how-inclusion-matters

74   Harvard Business Review Press, Williams, J.C. (2021). Bias Interrupted:
        Creating Inclusion For Real and For Good.

75   McKinsey & Co, "Diversity Wins: How Inclusion Matters,
        https://www.mckinsey.com/featured-insights/diversity-and-
        inclusion/diversity-wins-how-inclusion-matters

CHAPTER 6

PAGE   REFERENCE

83   Harvard Business Review, "How Hair Discrimination Affects Black
        Women at Work", https://hbr.org/2023/05/how-hair-discrimination-
        affects-black-women-at-work

CHAPTER 7

PAGE   REFERENCE

93   Organizational Behavior and Human Decision Processes,
        https://store.hbr.org/product/hbr-guide-to-dealing-with-conflict/10068

94   Conflict Resolution Playbook, Jeremy

Pollack,   https://www.amazon.com/Conflict-Resolution-Playbook-Communication-Preventing/dp/1647399521

CHAPTER 8

PAGE   REFERENCE

112   NeuroLeadership Institute, "A Tale of Three Allies: What Does Allyship Look Like in Real Life?" https://neuroleadership.com/your-brain-at-work/allyship-in-real-life/#:~:text=Acts%20of%20allyship%20generally%20fall,amplifying%20underappreciated%20perspectives%20and%20contributions.

112   Heartshift Collective, "Guide to Allyship", https://guidetoallyship.com

113   Harvard Business Review, "Creating Psychological Safety for Black Women at Your Company", https://hbr.org/2023/05/creating-psychological-safety-for-black-women-at-your-company

113   Textio, "Language Bias in Performance Feedback: 2022 Data Analysis and Survey Results", https://explore.textio.com/feedback-bias?submissionGuid=649821b6-2adf-4d2a-b323-aacf73020dc0

Andrew Adeniyi

AAA SOLUTIONS

AAA Solutions is a Black-owned and Black-led consulting firm that specializes in workplace culture and diversity, equity & inclusion (DEI). AAA Solutions provides audits and assessments, management consulting, strategic planning, and training services to small to medium sized businesses and non-profits. AAA Solutions is comprised of a team of empathetic problem solvers who serve as strategic advisors and thought partners to clients. We are on a mission to help leaders create more engaged, diverse, equitable, and inclusive cultures. Our core values are simplicity, autonomy, and growth. We are authorized partners of Everything DiSC by Wiley and The Five Behaviors of a Team by Patrick Lencioni. We leverage data and storytelling to reduce turnover, improve employee engagement, and increase productivity.

Contact Us

AAA Solutions
https://www.aaasolutions.us
Email: aaa@andrewadeniyi.com
317-207-6163

Andrew Adeniyi

Andrew Adeniyi

9 7 9 8 9 8 8 9 7 3 8 7 4